A NAME FOR EVIL

Books by ANDREW LYTLE

AT THE MOON'S INN
THE LONG NIGHT

A Name for Evil

A NOVEL BY

ANDREW LYTLE

THE BOBBS-MERRILL COMPANY

INDIANAPOLIS   *Publishers*   NEW YORK

To Edna

A NAME FOR EVIL

CHAPTER ONE

*W*HEN I saw the house I said, "The lines are good. It is in bad repair, but it will suit my purpose all the better." Its decay was not such that it was beyond restoration. Perhaps I should say regeneration, for I had bought more than a house. There was land attached and because land has history, is history rather, involving lives and fateful happenings, it is more exact to say regeneration. I ignored this fact, looking over the house with her that fall afternoon and talking excitedly over the problems which the abuse of indifferent tenants and croppers had caused, in their brutish way emphasizing the neglect of the owners. How sad, I reflected, and how evil a thing it is, to let a noble establishment be put into the hands of the depraved who care only for draining the land of its strength, always taking out, never putting back the food of life! But at the moment I must confess it was the house which occupied me. In spite of the decay it was beautiful on that day, a day bright and cool with the first dry breath of autumn. How much I would have spared us all, had I faced logically the entire meaning of the ruin we were about to enter and make our own!

I am convinced now there are certain places which

the past holds, literally, absolutely, and with a tenure no present occupant can dispute. I do not pretend to understand the metaphysics of such a lien, but I have felt its power. I do not speak now of the grosser illusion of ghosts with chains and such tommyrot, and yet who can say that even they, in all their melodramatic clanking, do not exist? What forms of being, what substances, do we not today accept, which once the wisest opinion would have denied? Man's brain, whirling in the vacuum it creates, precipitates from nothing the once hidden secrets of the universe. I smile as I use the word. Even the laws of the universe in this dark crucible must find another definition.

At some remote time the farm had belonged to my family, not to my immediate forebears, but to a collateral branch of the Revolutionary major who "removed," as the saying went, to the current West of the time. There have been so many Wests in our national life it puzzles me no end why historians take so little account of the true meaning of this remarkable circumstance. Unhappily our scholarship took for model the nineteenth-century German method of objectivity with all its sterile accumulation of data for data's sake. So many sins, public and private, have been disguised by pseudoscientific jargon. Like the mole underground the scholars dug and they dug, in their blindness through their dark tunnel. And the historian most of all reflected this infatuation. To write straight English prose made him suspect among his fellows. To show

10

imagination—that was professional suicide. The West, the progression of Wests: could he not see that there was more than accident to this repetition? The word, the faith rather of it, always in the American consciousness, the last resort of the desperate in fortune and body, what could it mean but one thing? To yearn for the West is simply to yearn for death. Why was it given to me, to me alone, to understand it like a prophet and to suffer it like a martyr?

I had just left Ellen somewhere in the house. The tenant's wife had given us permission to go through it, too obligingly I thought, or rather I didn't think. I only felt the woman's manner. But I paid her no mind, for I was enthralled with my wife's enthusiasm and her light gay movements about the dirty, scarred rooms. The wallpaper was torn from the walls, the plaster cracked and written upon, the edges of the floors painted the most horrid color of yellow; and where there wasn't the grime of years, the tenants' filthy disorder made even the grime look respectable. Through this Ellen sailed like an angel, exclaiming over the impressive woodwork, the winding stair, all the good points which she and I would revive for our own ends. I had never admired or loved her more than on that day. Her lovely little feet fairly seduced me all over again. There was something, as my father had said, about her gait. If he could have seen her then, he would have known it was the gait of a thoroughbred.

11

Disorder and ruin fascinate yet depress me. I felt the need for air and perspective and so went out into the yard. Soon I was busy at the problems before us. A small passageway between the kitchen and the main dwelling had been closed. This must be knocked out to restore the charm of covered ways meant to protect servants from the weather. The roof needed painting, window sills had rotted away, blinds were hanging askew or missing entirely; but I told myself that these were superficial things after all. The house, built of solid brick, was surely sound. How long it took me to finish these calculations I have no way of knowing. I merely wandered to the front of the house, thinking Ellen would be there. She was not there. This seemingly trivial fact contained for us the mystery of all fatality. It gave the slight jar to the door which even then was closing to shut us off from the natural world. The fateful moments of life are never discerned as they occur. Nor are they ever dramatic. At best they count as unimportant trifles to be brushed aside or forgotten. But later, when it is too late, we see them for what they are: signposts. It is for this reason they go unnoted. A sign points the way. It makes no comment on the end of the journey.

I called Ellen's name. The tenant's wife came to the door and said, "Ellen's in here."

I looked at her coldly. "Whom do you mean?" I asked. "Mrs. Brent?"

I felt both anger and pity for the woman. The

unique triumph of universal education is the successful way it debases the mind. Besides making the ig-
norant arrogant, this spun sugar of our political car-
nival has corrupted manners. A little understanding
of reading, writing, and ciphering caused this poor
woman—I do not overlook her feeling of injustice, but
alas, if one seeks justice . . . —to assert her feeling of
inferiority by assuming a social familiarity which
doesn't come by paying the poll tax. If she had been
called on to justify herself, she would have said, "She
ain't no better'n me." To this has come Jefferson's
dream and to this the lifting of a political phrase out
of the context of its time. In God's sight we are all
equal, but God's intentions are inscrutable. In the
blindness of the world there is no alternative to good
manners but brute force.

As we were driving away I said to Ellen, "I told
the tenant he would have to find another place."

"But I thought you were going to let him stay on?"

I then explained to her my reasons. Her voice
hastened, "But it is too late to trade for another
year."

"I will find someone."

"But if you don't, we can't afford to let the farm
lie idle and we are not ready to move."

"If the worst comes to the worst, we can take over,"
I said confidently.

"But the house—we can't live in it as it is."

"We won't be living. We'll camp at first and see

13

it change under our hands. I think that would be rather fun."

"Fun?" She queried. "There's no waterworks . . . no . . . no bathroom."

"Mighty good people made out all their lives without a bathroom. We ought to for a while."

"I know, but, darling . . ."

"Now, don't you worry your pretty head about this. I'll fix it."

She was silent as we drove back to town.

CHAPTER TWO

*A*s it turned out, Ellen's appre-
hensions were justified. I could
not find a tenant who would take
over responsibility for the farm. I did find a Negro
family who had been associated with the place for
many generations. This family moved in that winter,
but we waited until early spring. To try to live in the
house over the hard winter months would have exposed us to unnecessary hardship. After all *The Grove,*
for so the place was called, was to serve us, not we it.

We arrived one day in early spring to take formal
possession.

"Are you sure this is what you want?" Ellen was
asking.

We had just stopped the car in front of the house
and were looking at it. We had not alighted. We sat
in silence, I at the wheel and she beside me. I replied
irritably, or perhaps my voice carried a conviction that
was rather forced. "Of course this is what I want," I
said. And then as if to press her as an accomplice,
"Don't you want to do it? We've talked and planned
of a place all our own, a sort of base. Well, you've
got to have a place to keep your books."

"I was only thinking," she said.

15

"Thinking of what?"

"It's going to take a lot of money and a lot of work. I thought . . ."

"Yes?" I was a little impatient.

"Only that we ought to be sure."

"Of course we are sure," I said and got out of the car.

I slammed the door harder than I meant to.

She came to me and slipped her arm through mine. I pressed her to me for an instant. I did not understand my mood. I felt as if I had been put on the defensive and that my defense was false. This made me irritable, for there was no apparent reason for it. Nothing had occurred to make me change my mind, but as I stood on the broad lawn and looked through the old ragged cedars at the dwelling, I involuntarily pressed Ellen's arm into my side. We had seen *The Grove* many times, in fact and in the mind's eye, but we had never seen it empty before. The sloven Blacks—that was the name of the tenants I had ejected—gave it a certain if sorry kind of life. Well, life is scarcely the word. They had never lived there in the sense that you make a house reflect your being. Nor was it merely that they were slipshod tenants. I have seen croppers turn a shack into a livable and thriving scene of domestic well-being. The Blacks had done little better than camp at the place. Now gone, they could no longer divert me from seeing the truth. It was this truth which held my eyes and fixed me to the spot. *The Grove* did not look empty! Even

16

in its forlorn condition it gave all the appearance of having a life of its own. What this might be I, in my ignorance, could not decide. But in a few short seconds this much of my feeling had clarified itself : whatever this life was, it was to become ours too.

With this thought in mind I turned to Ellen. I turned with the abruptness of the descent of this knowledge. "Come, darling," I said with spirit, "I must carry you over the threshold."

"No, you don't," she answered playfully but pushing me away all the same. "You've carried me over two thresholds already."

I tried to grab her but she raced across the lawn, under the great cedars and up to the entrance doorway. She pulled open the heavy walnut door and sidled in. "Wait for me," I cried and ran after her, but before I could reach the top step, the door slowly swung to between us.

I grasped the knob. It was old brass and probably rusty. I grabbed it, turned it, but the door remained fast. Nervously I shook it, shaking, and calling her name. She did not answer. I set my face against the long red glass, those happy inventions of a day of much visiting, cast to give the host that moment of advantage, after the knocker falls, when he may look out but the guest may not look in. The redness of the glass blurred the long entrance hall, and the winding stair wavered as objects do under water, but Ellen I did nowhere see. I had only to run to the back of the house to enter, but I felt drawn to that door.

Through that door alone I would enter and find my wife. It was ridiculous. The day was overcast and coldish, as are so many early spring days, but it was ten o'clock in the morning. Men were turning the land. In the field to the side of the house two dogs were chasing a rabbit, and yet I felt that to separate my hand from that tarnished brass knob would set me adrift on a tow which would sweep me forever away from the safe known into the swirling pools of strangeness. I made a lurch at the knob—you can see how far gone I was in hysteria—when at my ear a voice said, "Excuse me, sir, I'll unlock d' door for you."

"But it isn't locked," I almost shouted.

The Negro bent down and slipped the old key into its lock, making the necessary movement into a bow, with just the proper inclination of his head in my direction. In that short time I managed to compose myself so that I was fairly calm as he stepped back.

"You can enter now," he said gravely, handing me the key. "Them folks give it to me when they removed."

"Thank you, Johnny," I replied more easily. "Miss Ellen went in before me. I could not understand how the door locked itself."

He made no response to this but presented me the blank mask of patience and reserve which with Negroes of a certain generation seems to imply a secret commentary.

Once inside I hurried through empty rooms, each

18

one flashing its peculiar mark of decay and abuse . . . paper hanging from the walls, the stain of rain, old rags thrust through a window light. I hurried on, into the dining room, its grime and grease thick on the floor and splashed about the wainscoting near the mantel. The rusty flue mouth gaped obscenely. Charred holes gouged the floor where the Blacks and others like the Blacks had set the cookstove. It was the well-swept floors which set off these marks of debased living. Johnny had followed my directions. I noted this even in my distraction, for the landlord can tell by the way the new tenant reacts to his orders how well they will get on together.

But in none of these rooms did I find Ellen. I waited until I had got out of hearing of the hall and called. It was important not to be surprised again in Johnny's hearing. "Ellen!" My voice sounded no louder than an urgent whisper. "Ellen, Ellen" went before me up the back stairs and through the upper rooms of the L. But no reply did I get to an appeal become too desperate for the occasion. My alarm was absurd, yet for all its absurdity, how real!

The particular charm of the place lay in its L. The house itself was the usual multiple of the dog run, raised to imposing proportions, hall above and below, with four bedrooms of enormous size opening on the upper hall and attached to each room a small cabinet for dressing. Near the front of the upper hall a passage opened onto a long narrow gallery, with brick arches supporting the roof. This gallery repeated itself on the other side, so that one might walk entirely around the three small rooms, all in a row and opening to either view. Each room stood at a level lower than the one above, causing you to step down the arched way until you came to the bottom level. Here the gallery separated the end room from the other two. In this room I found Ellen.

The door stood open. A moment passed before she gave any sign of recognition. On seeing me, she started slightly. "Why, darling, you seem all in a fuss," she said, smiling sweetly and coming forward.

"Didn't you hear me call?"

"Call?" she returned with a winning innocence. How well and perfect was her surprise at the quality of alarm still in my voice! And truly now my alarm seemed foolish enough and I found I had nothing to say. As if sensing my embarrassment, she chattered in the thoroughly natural way of a good housekeeper. "Whoever cleaned up," she said, "gave out when they got here. Look. Nothing has been swept in this room. The dirt is inches deep."

"I'll speak to Johnny about this," I said and laughed heartily, too heartily, as it seemed to her, for the occasion. She looked at me with a queer expression. Naturally my sudden burst of laughter seemed strange to her, but I could not explain without alarming her or else seeming more foolish in her eyes. Neither did I want to do. And indeed my fears now seemed altogether fantastic, and having nothing to say, I grew

20

silent once more. Ellen in her wonderfully tactful way began to speak.

"Look," she said enthusiastically. "We can make this entire upper L into our apartment. We will glass in the arches. One room shall be our bedroom. One an upstairs sitting room. That of course will really be mine, but we will call it ours. And this room—" she looked slowly about it—"dust and all, shall be your study."

"Fine," I responded with enthusiasm to match hers. "It is here we will begin the restoration."

Why, I do not know, but I said it like a challenge.

CHAPTER THREE

*T*HE feeling, premonition, call it whatever you will—certainly it had no logical genesis—I had had before the door to the entrance hall stayed with me. Not that I brooded on it, nor even thought about it. It had entered my blood, changing its chemistry, diffused, unseen, awaiting the catalytic agent which would precipitate it, when it would appear in all the awful isolation of its elemental state.

I recall the busy weeks of this period, when I was both aware and unaware of the approaching connection of events so dire that now I wonder how, for a moment, I misread the signs. There was the small matter of the unswept room, trivial enough in itself and easily explained: the house was big and the sweeper or sweepers had merely overlooked the small room at the end of the L's second story. I should have forgotten it by payday, as indeed I forgot it during the interval; but as I made out the pay check it came to me to say, so casually there was not the slightest hint of what I sought, "By the way, Johnny, they didn't sweep the little room upstairs."

My statement was met by silence, so that I had to repeat myself. I did this deliberately, to take the proper strategic position to force from him the true reason for the neglect. Johnny's silence had told me what I had suspected: the room had not been ignored for any of the obvious reasons. I unbent somewhat and said in my most pleasant manner, "Come now, Johnny, what was the reason?" As I spoke, I looked directly at him, to let him know I would not laugh or assume an attitude by which he would lose dignity. He returned my look with the degree of confidence I had invited.

"That's old Major Brent's room," he answered.

There was no apology in the muddy white of his eyes. Nor in his voice. His speech was a statement, and he spoke it as if it were self-explanatory. But I did not let him off so easily.

"What do you mean, Major Brent's room? He's been dead seventy-five years."

"He a hard man. He don't like folks projecting wid his things."

"So you believe in ghosts?" I asked with reproving humor.

In a most polite way he followed the line of his evasion. "When he a old man, he stand on the porch there, in the dark, and ring the bell. And his boys better waste no time gitten up. He drove them hard as he drove he hands. He stand there and lay out the work for the day, work most folks take three days to do. He say, 'No triflen. If you kill a mule, I'll buy another. If you kill a Negro, I'll buy another.' And they say, 'Yessir, Pa.' Then he go upstairs to he room, and we all knowed he had eyes like a crow."

I waited before I spoke again. Then I leaned forward. "But, Johnny, you weren't living then."

"No, sir," he replied, with the proper deference for the amenities, and then resumed, "If us'ud stop at the end of the row to blow a spell, he tap the bell. We knowed what dat meant. The sun was sizzlen hot and the clods hot to our feets and our bref dried out our moufs, but didn't nobody tarry. Not here. No, sir, not here dey didn't."

"But, Johnny," I said with a slight edge to my words, "that was years ago, before you or anybody in this country was born."

"Yessir," he said respectfully.

"Ghosts can't hurt you."

"No, sir," he agreed.

"Then why were you afraid to sweep my room."

"Major Brent don't allow nobody in there."

I was baffled. Johnny was not senile. He was not crazy. He had all the guile and simplicity of a country Negro, and I was certain he was a man of character. In spite of myself he had put me on the defensive. It was he, not I, who determined the limits of our talk. I either had to lose my temper, a bad thing always for the boss, or accept the fiction that old Major Brent had a kind of immortality attributed only to demigods. Certainly he could not be numbered among ghosts of the common garden variety.

I shifted ground and tried to get at Johnny another

way. I could not leave things as they were: that is, I could in no way accept the fiction his attitude would impose, the impossible position of allowing the spirit of a dead man to determine what would and would not be done at *The Grove*. At the same time I knew that I would fail if I had to come to grips with a superstition of such peculiar power. I had to recover control and I had to do it then and there. I thought fast. It did not take me a minute to reach a decision. I did what was left to do. I accepted the full measure of the challenge—a strange kind of engagement it was—between the living and the dead. I accepted it without hesitation and without reservations. My decision brought relief, as I raised my eyes and looked squarely at Johnny. "I am taking that little room for my study," I said and paused to let this information sink in. Then I added quietly, "Whoever occupied it in the past, be it man or spirit, can file no claim now. It is too late. Mine it is, and mine alone."

His expression did not change, but I saw that I had made my point and well made it. Seeing how my position had strengthened, I made it stronger still. "Of course, I can't occupy a dirty room. If your women are afraid of ghosts, I won't ask them to tend it." I could feel, oh with what joy I felt that I now held the reins! "If necessary," I said, "I'll sweep it myself." How well I had calculated I could see in the slight shift of the shoulders, a drooping and a straightening. Those few seconds told me much. He was not a servant who worked only for wages. That was the advantage I had over him. It was on that knowledge I gambled. He knew I could not be allowed to dust my own furniture. He said very simply, "I will tend the room."

I bowed slightly, to indicate that such would be agreeable to me; then to make the sure surer, to consolidate my already consolidated position, I spoke once more before he returned to the matter of farm business on which he had come. "You must know, Johnny, that if you look to a ghost for meat, your chin will get mighty dry." I was cool and reserved as I spoke, perhaps with a touch of humor, to soften the implied threat of my words. Then quickly I shifted the conversation.

I did this as much as anything to disguise my triumph, and it was no slight one. There would be no more of this business of referring to the dead as alive. Wryly I thought how nice it would be if old Major Brent would pay the taxes. A ghost was a perfectly recognizable myth. I could dispose of that. But a man who was immortal? That was not for me, not with all the other problems I had to confront. And so it came about that in my delight I allowed Johnny to choose what fields would be planted in tobacco, in grain, and in hay.

As he was turning away, he said, "I forgot to mention the corn ground. That field that lies next to the woods make mighty fine corn."

"Go ahead. Plant it," I said in the security of my triumph.

He put his hat on. "Major Brent likes his corn planted there," he said politely and, bowing slightly, walked away.

CHAPTER FOUR

*H*ow was I to take this parting statement? As insolence? I confess that was my first reaction. It took a while to quiet the anger in my heart, and killing anger it was. Only by great effort did I restrain myself as my blurred eyes watched him walk calmly away with my triumph. But reason prevailed, slowly as the pounding in my head eased its strokes. After all, I had to tell myself, I had given him permission to plant the corn where he chose. His comment was a small matter. This, at least, was the official view to take. For could not I have ordered the corn put elsewhere? If I was tricked into giving permission, it was I, the rightful owner and landlord, who had to be tricked. And so long as the duel kept to the rules, I was content. At least I would win or lose on my own merit and skill. But the more I turned Johnny's behavior over in my head the more I dismissed the idea of any intended insolence. He had been connected with *The Grove* longer than I. In his way he had shown respect for its tradition, certainly a virtue I should try to increase, not thwart. I was the interloper, the untried one. For almost the years of his life Johnny had seen owners and tenants abuse

house and land. It was to his honor that he kept faith
with the memory of Major Brent, the only man within
his knowledge who had brought *The Grove* to its
highest moment and then sustained it. In his tradi-
tion-respecting mind Johnny could find little help
from the dead. Countryman that he was, he was too
familiar with the natural order: the dead are dead. So
dramatically, and because of the drama to his mind
believable, he went beyond the laws of nature and
endowed the Major with the mystery of immortality
and its limitless prerogatives.

So I worked it out at the moment. In those days I
had skill in such matters. I prided myself on knowing people better than they knew themselves, and obviously the situation had to be solved or I was faced
with ruin. I could not actually farm the land myself;
I could not afford to lose a crop without endangering
all I had put into the venture, not to mention my
peace of mind, or Ellen's.

I am not a romantic. The true romantic has hidden
pockets into which his imagination secretes a drug to
protect him from the common evils of the hour. I
am, I was, that most unhappy of hybrids, the false romantic. With will and deliberation, and this is the
essence of the difference, the false romantic ignores
the true nature of reality. For the time being. And
in the beginning he knows it is only for the time being.
With care and half-averted eye he hangs the veil of
illusion between himself and the world. Almost from
habit he believes the veil was hung by God, or in the

most violent falsification of his nature, he becomes God. I say almost, for he never quite forgets what he is doing. There is this to be said for him. More often the injury done is to himself alone. The true romantic poisons the air all men breathe.

Later, in my study, where I threw myself on the couch, exhausted from the ordeal, I began to review my situation. How blithely I had gone into this business! And truly the idea had seemed sound: establish my family in one location as a safeguard against the hazards of my uncertain profession; regenerate a family place and make up for the failure in trusteeship of those who had gone before. Was this unduly romantic? There, on the couch in that little study, I seemed to myself no squatter but the proper kind of heir. And besides, how much more worth while, how much more manhood this undertaking demanded than to stay in town, spend our days in poker playing and entertaining casual drifters who came to us to fill their emptiness. What I had not foreseen was the magnitude of the undertaking. Both Ellen and I, she more than I, had had that moment of warning, standing there on the lawn when we had arrived to possess *The Grove*. This warning I refused to hear, and even now, when it sounded a second time and more clearly, for Johnny's obsession with the Founder was a line leading directly to the past—even now I might have withdrawn. Instead I rose to my feet and silently—for where was my adversary visible?—renewed the challenge. I would stay and fulfill my destiny.

And so the die was cast. It had been all along, but there is something final about deliberate choice, the act of will which saves or damns. In all good camaraderie Ellen and I set up our double bed in one of the large rooms downstairs. How bare the bed made the room seem, and how impermanent our occupancy! The fact that it was a temporary arrangement did not help much. We had moved in below so that we could work freely on the apartment upstairs. Each night I had to look up at the cracks in the ceiling, at the strips of torn and faded paper. In spite of myself I began to feel unclean, spiritually at first and then more directly. I noticed if I were not careful, my body took on a poor-white smell.

During these days I wondered again and again at Ellen's good sportsmanship. If I felt so, how must she feel? Her acceptance of a situation whose demands grew daily more complex brought from me nothing but admiration. Ordinarily a man does not care how things look, so long as he knows they will improve. But a woman of beauty, and Ellen's beauty was renowned, requires time to maintain it. There is the ritual of the hair, the hands, the exacting, oh so exacting art of make-up. There are the thousand and one things which a man does not understand but which a woman practices with the skill and discipline of an artist. In ordinary conditions the husband has little occasion to be aware of this endless effort to remain young and beautiful. But here, at *The Grove,* this effort made itself painfully apparent.

As I watched her cope with the unending chores of housekeeping in her impossible surroundings and the renovation of our ruined grandeur, I felt the sweet pain of pathos bite into me, for her and for all creatures trapped by circumstance. She was one of those rare beings nature creates by accident. There was in her constitution almost a biological lack—an inability to suffer what we all must suffer, the plain facts of living. I said to myself that the power which creates made her as an image for all men to behold, an image of inviolability to change. This was her given function. This and this above all. She was never, oh never, to endure the common filth of living. But that same power had set her in the way of the world as it might hurl the ideal bird into the air and forget to give it wings to fly.

Or so it seemed to me in my partial knowledge as I watched her slim figure, the small well-shod feet, the tailored look—for so she always appeared no matter what she wore—pass through the halls and rooms still showing the corrosion of time. I began to tremble, thinking of the day when the scales would drop from her eyes, that divine web which hid from her the vast complexity of our situation. This thought sent me into renewed activity, the haste that is always waste, the desperate compromise to get a thing done, no matter how. And to find that after the moral defeat which all compromises entail things were still undone, or only started to be dropped at the capricious hands of carpenters and plumbers.

How near my fears approached the thing feared showed in an incident which happened at the lunch hour in early June. I was always coming or going on diplomatic missions to workmen. I came in, from what errand I do not now remember, and found Ellen standing by the table we had set up on the porch. The porch, I must add, had been repaired but, like everything else I had had done, was still unfinished. She was in tears. She stood back from the table, pointing at it, her face set in a strain of horror beyond any obvious cause.

"Look!" she cried. "Just look!"

The tone of hysteria in her voice frightened me. Quickly I looked where she pointed; saw the food set out and nothing more. I raised my eyes with a question. "But, darling, what?"

"Those flies," she replied, in loathing and disgust.

"Flies?" I repeated stupidly.

"All morning I've worked hard in the kitchen to prepare a good lunch. Now look at it. It's ruined."

"Flies are bad," I said. "But nothing's ruined. It's the time of year for them." I tried to soothe her as best I could. "Come, I'll shoo them away. As soon as I can get the wire, I'll screen in this part of the porch. In time I'll move the barn."

She turned on me a look more of incomprehension than anger. "That's all you ever say, Henry. In time."

"Why, honey."

"You do nothing to make it easy for me. All day you ride around and walk in the fields and woods. I

33

do the drudgery." Her voice drew fine. "You don't know what I put up with. You don't care."

"I do care. You know I care. But there's a war on. It's hard to get things and get them done. I work at it every day, and I do care," I wound up. I thought I was magnificent in my restraint, but it brought me nowhere. She refused to eat with me or eat at all. She fled to our room in tears and shut herself in.

I had come in tired and hungry. Now my appetite was gone. I was also baffled and angry. My load was already as heavy as I could bear. To add to it in this way seemed unfair. The middle of a project is no time to judge it, nor judge me. So I felt, but I well knew that my feelings were beside the point. I turned away from the ruin of the meal, drew in my breath, and knocked at the door to our room.

She was sitting up in bed, her swollen eyes staring in utmost dejection.

"Darling, I'm sorry," I said. "I *will* make it better for you."

She seemed not to hear. In a pitiful, childlike way she lifted her hands and turned them over, as if she were seeing them for the first time.

"Look," she wailed, "how rough they are!"

I sat beside her and took her hands in mine and caressed them. But I could find no words for comfort. What was I to say? Your hands will grow smooth and white again? With no cook and no immediate prospect of help?

Suddenly, with fierce intention, she grasped my

34

hands. "Let's go away from this place. While there's time. We are young now. It will take years to make the house livable, even decent. Then it will be too late." Almost as an afterthought she added, "We will be old then. Old—and ugly."

"Try to be patient," I said.

That was all I could say. I felt foolish but there was desperation in my voice, for I was really saying, "Don't shake my faith in myself." My next words showed the full measure of my desperation. "What I am doing, Ellen, is for you."

"Henry Brent, no other man would ask a woman to live like this," she said at last.

Her words struck like a blow; then I was lost in the blank swoon of the heart in which, moments later, the meaning of her accusation rushed. This was not the frailty I had feared. This was much worse: a rift to make two of one, a blasphemy against the union of marriage, where common ends diverge. I had not foreseen it nor prepared for it. Nor was I now prepared. I could only stammer, "But you agreed."

"I have tried," she said disconsolately and then raised her hand in a vague gesture toward the room.

My eyes followed. The hot midday sun was streaming through the curtainless windows, leaving not a shadow to soften or disguise the room's bleak and sordid appearance. In one upper corner long brown streaks, the color of tobacco spittle, stained the wall. And everywhere the endless plaster cracks. In one corner sat a trunk piled with clothes. A lone chair

faced the cheerless hearth, a thing of pure utility with
no promise of domestic comfort. But nothing pointed
out the bleakness of our situation so dramatically as
the bilious-colored paint that once had outlined the
rug. I don't know why, but the bare middle of the
floor contained for me at that moment the most violent
threat to our venture: nay—to our life even.

At last I looked up, to face it out with Ellen. Erect,
with her hands folded on the counterpane and tightly
clasped, she sat withdrawn, immobile, straining into
a stilled image, as if to move would open her body to
the contagious air. What struck me most was her out-
of-placeness in the room and also, in spite of her complaint about her hands, the certainty that the decay
around us would never spread to her person or to her
will. It might destroy, it would never claim her. I
looked more closely and already saw marks of the
struggle. Her old radiance had gone out of her, but
she was still lovely to look at; and where all was sordid, she shone pure, trim, and immaculate. Shone
was the word, but the light she gave off no longer
came from an inner source. It was all surface reflection.

And there she was and there I was, in the full flood
of high noon, mere flecks in the hot speed of the sun, its
rush a bright stillness from window to window until the
solid brick walls all seemed of glass. In self-pity and
sorrow for creature kind I understood how along this
burning way time fused with space, how there was
neither motion nor surface but endless extension into

which all was lost. I understood the feeble valiant
effort of builders to raise walls against this burning
force which in giving life made it ignominious. Instinctively I went to her and took her in my arms and lay
between her and the bright glare. She misunderstood
my intention and pushed me away. "Don't," she said
harshly. "Can't you see we have no privacy here?"

CHAPTER FIVE

I TRIED to shut out the memory of this incident by redoubling my efforts. And during the following weeks I was up early and to bed late. Of course there was no time for my own proper work. Money was constantly going out and little coming in, but the house did show improvement. The back porch got screened in and painted, and our apartment upstairs was well under way, all except my office which I kept until last. That I would do alone. The wonder of it all was the way Ellen's spirits rose as the things got done. She seemed to have recovered entirely from her "breakdown," as she called it. She had even come to me and told me she would not let herself get out of hand again. My spirits rose too from this happy condition of our affairs, although there was a qualification to what I felt. Underneath this surface of good will and good heart I could feel from time to time the tremors of the earth we, so to speak, stood on. Well, the quake of which they were the forewarning was not long in coming.

My ear was to the ground, but I had allowed myself to drift into the state of hearing without translating the meaning of what I heard. I merely stored away the recordings without comment in that part of the mind

38

where records are kept. Ellen's pleasure in what had been done blinded me to how little it was in relation to what we still had to do. There were as well growing doubts in my mind as to whether we would ever be able to complete the house's regeneration. The cost was mounting and fast mounting beyond my capacity to pay. If it was to be finished, we would have to do of necessity what once had seemed a labor of love: that is, do a great part of the work ourselves. This would take years out of our life and make of these years confusion and disorder, for a house must be so arranged that there is a place for everything. How could a well-ordered ménage function with everything topsy-turvy, with tools and lumber all over and debris scattered about? To set up the rooms as they were for living was out of the question. In the urgency of the daily crisis we would have to put off until the suitable time (which never comes) our intended restoration, until at last like the tenants who had gone before we would grow accustomed to our surroundings and carry a step farther, because of our corruption, the progress of ruin.

So Ellen's first gloomy prophecy in the light of the actual situation seemed truer than her more recent optimism. Even if by some miracle we brought the house to its former state, could we produce the conditions which had sustained it? Servants are as necessary to a large establishment as bread to the body. These might conceivably be obtained, but would the land sustain them? *The Grove* at its heyday was a going concern in every way. No money was brought in from the outside to run it. The land maintained the economy of the house, its hospitality and gracious living. But since those days the country has become an extension of the town. Let us be frank. It is servile. Its mores, the price it gets for its products, the clothes it wears, almost what it thinks, are determined by an absentee master. You may name this master what you please. It matters little whether its elusive all-powerful mechanism is controlled by management or by labor. On either horn the farmer is gored. So among the many difficulties to be solved and got out of the way was the insoluble one of history.

But sufficient unto the day is the evil thereof. On this old saw I lived and moved, dealing with whatever situation came up, putting it through or compromising it, and enjoying the respite it gave us both. Late at night we would talk of the progress made that day and of the things still to do, or more often we fell into bed too weary for words and stumbled out at light to take up whatever came to hand. And so our life went at *The Grove,* swiftly, pleasantly, as only it can go when two people who love each other, who have quarreled and made up, are doing things together. That it was slow, that it was little, that the means to prosecute it were fast diminishing, lay like shadows at high noon, which the eye wonders at but dismisses in the bright swelter of the hour.

The very brightness of this period, as I try to recall it, seems brief enough, scarcely more than a flash before the gloom which settled down. I remember no clear division between the night and the day of our ordeal. The change came suddenly, like the turning out of a light. What followed was the endless groping in the dark, when the familiar landmarks of the room turn strange, and the terror is greater for the knowledge that all you touch should be familiar. The darkness then seems no longer confined but the very core of night's wide spaces.

Often during this time I found myself thinking of my predecessor. I can call him that, for those who dwelt at *The Grove* between his time and mine might as well have never lived for any thought I gave them. I thought of him with envy and sometimes almost with hatred, for he had had all I was denied. I could almost see him beyond the grave willing me to make him immortal. *The Grove* was his conception. It bore the stamp of his mind and his will. And his mind and his will *I* was restoring and the better I did it the more I submerged my personality and the greener his kept. If into his habitation I could have established my family after the fashion of my hopes, I could have mocked him. The probability of my failure and his success haunted me. Was he really a better man than I? Could I in his place and in his time have done as well? Could he have coped with the situation, if our roles had been reversed? I could never make up my mind to these questions. At times I fell back on the frail comfort that I had undertaken an impossible job. But always the element of doubt crept in to plague me, for given any set of limitations one man will succeed where another fails.

The Grove had one feature which somehow had escaped the careless hands that had misguided so much else. It was the way the lawn sloped away from the house until it lost itself in a fine woods. Ellen and I had formed the habit, when the going got especially tough, of walking away from our troubles into the cool green spaces, where we strolled for hours on end. And always we returned refreshed to the battle. One evening about dusk, coming from the fields with the day's work behind, I passed through these woods on the way to the house. As I stepped out onto the lawn, I came instinctively to a dead stop. I say instinctively, but even now I do not know whether at first I felt or saw what confronted me. In one of the arches of the upper gallery stood the figure of a man. It stood in the arch which framed the door leading into the room we were doing over for Ellen. The house was a fair distance away, but through the cedars, as one must see it from my position, it appeared farther than it was. So it happened I could not quite make out the person's features. My first impression was that it was some guest looking over our improvements. I waved my hand and hurried across the lawn to greet him. When we first moved to the country, many of our acquaintances and friends made trips to see us. Their curiosity once satisfied they rarely braved the bad roads to make a second visit. But they were always welcome and so I went forward with pleasant anticipations. At that time of day objects are clear enough but the detail is blurred; so I had gone a little way before two things came to me, as

42

it happened, almost instantaneously: one, that my greeting had not been returned; and two, that there was no car in the driveway by which a guest could have arrived.

The shock of this double surprise slowed my steps and I came again to a halt. As I try now to remember it, the shock I felt was not at first very great. It was more a feeling of things being not quite right. It never occurred to me at the moment to wonder how this man got on the upper gallery. I assumed that he had made himself known to Ellen and had given her a satisfactory explanation of his business there, or she would not have let him in. Our situation was remote enough, so that I felt little danger from the gentlemen of no location who wander the highways. We were definitely on a byway; still I had warned her to be circumspect about strangers. If they happened upon us all the more reason for caution, since their mere presence would demand a clear explanation. What changed almost in a breath my puzzlement to alarm came out of, or made, the chill in the air which tightened my skin and made it tingle with fear. I had stopped beneath one of the giant cedars and from this position I had a direct and unimpeded view of the house. I could see and what I saw intensified my feeling of things not being right to a positive knowledge of something being very wrong. What I got first on the rebound was the certainty that I had never before seen the figure who was making himself so free of my house. As this struck me, it also struck me that he had all the air of one whose right to be where he was could never be questioned. The synthesis of the eye makes the analysis of statement slow and cumbrous, so that what I now report in detail misconstrues by the limitations of print the exact intensity of the emotions which fixed me to the spot.

My first impulse was to call out; but, realizing that he had not yet seen me, I took advantage of this to spy on him. I suppose this was my intention. It may have been I needed time to collect my wits. I know I froze as animals do when they sense danger, swallowed up by the frightful quiet which seemed all the more sinister for being a grotesque mockery of the dying away, the closing up of sound, common to the day's end. But the quiet into which I had sunk, which made my breath seem gross and noisy, although I scarcely breathed, was the quiet of the wave's trough or that moment of breathlessness when a high wind shuts off suddenly to gather itself for greater fury.

Across the space which joined us I tried to catch his gaze moving slowly in my direction. But it passed above me as if I were not there, pausing not even for an instant of recognition, all the while restlessly scanning the woods behind me. How can I say how long this took? Time passed, but also my recognition of it. This I know, time enough for me to see him so clearly as to make friends of a lifetime seem shadowy strangers passed in the street. I saw that he wore a hat—widebrimmed and black—but no tie or collar. One hand grasped a staff, the other hung at his side. There was no movement of neck or head, only the lustrous eyes,

44

restless, searching, boring the woods like gimlets.

My intolerable situation pressed on me I opened my mouth to call out, but even as I did so, he turned away and deliberately, as if he knew the way, walked in the direction of my study. He passed behind an arch. I waited the seconds it would take him to come out on the other side. I waited. I strained my eyes. All to no purpose. He passed behind the arch. He did not come out on the other side.

CHAPTER SIX

ONE does not reckon time at such moments, but when I ran for the house I had the feeling that I had waited too long. In one step I was on the porch. Another took me into the hall. I bounded up the stairs and down the drops of the gallery porch. Nothing did I see. Cautiously I put my hand on the knob of the door to my study and flung it back. What I would have done had I surprised a vicious marauder I cannot say, for I had not stopped to pick up even a stick. Luckily, or unluckily—the edge of truth is finely drawn in such contingencies—I faced an empty room. I looked all through it, behind the door, into closets meant for bookcases, I looked under my desk, but in all this frenzied search I found just what I knew I would find—nothing.

I told myself I must be thorough. There was the upstairs apartment to go through. No opportunity for doubt must be left lurking in my consciousness to trouble me, now that the swell of what I had felt growing about us at *The Grove* had at last exploded in my face. I had lost that first charge of fear. Almost I felt a deep relief, a kind of courage I never knew I had. Here was something which would call up to the very last reserve my manhood. No more plumbers and carpenters, no more painters and paper hangers to try the patience of a dozen Jobs. Here was drama, with the first act started, and the protagonist on the stage.

I ran into Ellen outside my door. By now the world had reached the division between night and day, those few short minutes when the sky has just enough light to show up the dark, before it closes in. The moment we met I noticed she was a little out of breath, but what drove all else away was the look of her face. By reflection I saw how I must have appeared to her. "What in the world is the matter?" she asked.

"Do I look that bad?"

"Terrible, Henry."

"Terrible?" I was playing for time.

"You look like a ghost."

I looked at her sharply. "And how does a ghost look? Have you ever seen one?"

"Don't be silly. Come on down to supper before it ruins."

Her words made me certain that I alone at <i>The Grove</i> had seen the intruder. I had sensed this fact, if you will, even before she appeared on the gallery. But what occupied me at the moment, as I hung back, was whether to tell her or keep my counsel. I was not long in reaching a decision. It came to me in one of those flashes of intuition which predetermine strategy that Ellen must not know. At least not for the present, certainly not until I had had time to reflect, to sound the depths of whatever waters we were treading. This meant of course that I could not at that moment search

47

the upstairs apartment. But, at once I reflected, there is the back stairs which opened an easy and quick escape. The visitor no doubt had already, had in fact before I arrived on the scene, disappeared into the anonymous regions from which he had come. So with alacrity I took Ellen's hand and led her down to supper. I went with the more willingness because I carried away one unshaken conviction. I would not be too late next time.

The strangest result of the whole encounter, among the numerous possibilities it opened up, was my part in it: that is, the change which came over me. It was the exact opposite to what one might have expected. My anxiety, my frustrations, all my gloomy preoccupations with my problem, every one of them left me. The business which had plagued me, had sent me endless miles on fruitless errands, still existed. The need to keep at it was no less urgent than it had been. The house still showed its state of limited repair, the farm work still moved on its original halting lines; the shift from a romantic preconception to actuality continued to rule our lives. Nothing had changed, and yet I had. All of this bothered me not at all. I was like a man aroused from the sleep of haunting dreams to a fair, brisk, and sunny day. And yet the reverse of all this came nearer the truth. I imitated Pilate. I did not examine the truth; I washed my hands of it.

How shall I describe the ensuing days? In this wonderful, almost miraculous, metamorphosis of feeling, of attitude, even of temperament which I had undergone, I let the problems which were arising daily more or less work themselves out. And work themselves out they did, after a fashion. This allowed me time for Ellen's society. It was only then, in the happy moments we spent together, that I understood how lonely she had been and how empty of the smaller pleasures my endless trips had made her life.

With Johnny's help we spent several weeks finishing the apartment. He could spare certain days from farm work as he had three stout boys to help make his crop. Except for a local paper hanger and a cabinetmaker of some skill we did the entire job ourselves. I was particularly proud of the floors. These fell to me. I rented a sander, worked them down, filled them, steel-wooled them, shellacked them, steel-wooled them again, and finally waxed and polished them. I have been rapid in the telling of it, but it was the hardest work I have ever done in all my life, and it was worth it. The floors were of wide ash boards, and when I got through they shone like satin. We rather splurged on the rugs and draperies, taking the money laid aside for the whole upstairs. As I report it here, we seemed madly extravagant, but we had set ourselves high standards. The house deserved the best and with complete agreement we decided to do what we did well, even if it took years to whip the interior into shape.

I still think this was the only way, the bold way, to approach our problem. Could we be held to account if we fell into the error of judgment common to all doers-over of old houses—underestimating the cost? I think not. With the apartment in such shape that an honest decorator would find little to criticize we had established a strong point inside the enemy's lines. Within the walls of the three rooms we could follow the small but so important habits of civilized living. To this sanctuary we could retire, bind up our wounds, and rest. And from here we could return refreshed to the battle. With this surely gained, what was to keep us from extending ourselves so that gradually we would set to rights the chaos of ruin everywhere about? What indeed? This was the question I asked in the days to come and from every side approached for an answer.

CHAPTER SEVEN

*B*EFORE I get on, it would be well to pause and catch, so to speak, my imaginative breath. I must be sure that what I now relate has above all the correct emphasis. If I have forgotten the order, if I have misunderstood the least step, even, in the progress of events so rapidly advancing toward their fulfillment, I place myself in the way of fresh perils. Only this time the perils are quite definitely of the soul. Never before has the risk of judgment so involved the risk of damnation, for if the truth I now disclose be not the truth but falsehood disguised in the habiliments of innocence, what then am I?

Doing things together brought us, as I thought, so close together that it made out of companionship a lovely harmony which is often lacking in married couples well away from the apprenticeship of the honeymoon. We felt as do people who, thinking they have lost a fortune, prepare for the dark dread of poverty only to discover that the fortune risked, instead of being lost, has returned tenfold. The evidence of this would seem commonplace enough—no more than the comforts and petty luxuries of civilized needs which the apartment now allowed us, or rather gave back

tremendously enhanced in value by the recent depriva-
tion we had suffered. How shall I put it? The excite-
ment and relief we shared will seem all out of proportion to the material value of our possessions. They
were, indeed, little more than what a good salaried man
in this preposterously wealthy country might command.
There were soft rugs at our feet instead of dusty floors.
There were curtains, beautiful to be sure, hanging at
our windows. But who lacks curtains? We had a fine
old bed, inherited but done over at our expense and with
good springs, but still any traveling salesman might
sleep as well.

We did have the advantage of Ellen's taste, and we
did have something to work with which gave our quarters a distinction all the chromium plate in the world
couldn't match. And at last we could keep the rooms
clean. In the rest of the house this was a backbreaking
job and one which got us nowhere. For all the sweep-
ing, dust, that sign of abandonment, persisted. But
now we passed from Ellen's room into her sitting room
on clean beautiful floors, and from there across the corridor to my room. My room was less extravagantly
done over; yet it *was* done over. But above all this our
situation had a very special quality: on the one hand
there was the apartment, on the other the rest of the
house. In this sentence I have posited two worlds. The
apartment allowed us to go on. It had blessed privacy.
It was at times our refuge. It would come to have the
grim tension of an embattled fortress.

One of the many disillusionments in which are contained the successive small shocks of life is the habit of growing accustomed to what falls your way. So it was that before many days I grew somewhat accustomed to the apartment. I modify this rather unctuous pronouncement by "somewhat," for the tremendous difficulties of our undertaking never let me take our gains too complacently. This produced in me a curious reaction. There were moments when I was acutely sensitive to our predicament, but most of the time I wandered about in a state of lethargy. Ellen had plans for the kitchen and dining room, but she could not rouse me to tackle them. I always put her off. Looking back on it, I can best describe my state of mind as that of one anxious to enjoy the newness of accomplishment before it dulled. I felt, if I felt anything, that there was time for the rest—of course there is never time—or perhaps I felt I must allow nothing to disturb the exquisite pleasure of being with Ellen and having the leisure to satiate myself with her company in surroundings at last proper to her beauty and grace. I would sit in a comfortable chair, with my leg thrown over its arm and watch her at her toilet. I feasted my eyes not as an adolescent who eats until he cloys, gulping down the senses when they are keenest, but with a more deliberate taste. And yet for the moment I had restored my senses to an acute freshness, while practicing the melancholy ritual of enjoyment, knowing it would not last. At times it seemed enough merely to watch her pass across the room. She had a dressing gown, I remember, of some thin blue stuff over pink, which clung to her or fell away as she walked, confusing the eye with the delicate change of color. Out from under it moved her little feet. Usually I was aware only of their positive outward thrusts. But one day my eyes fastened on them to enjoy their singularity. I saw the slippers she wore, woven leather of gold and silver gilt, sink into the deep new nap of the rug. The slippers were old and tarnished. Suddenly, as if I might defend her against this warning of our predicament, I took her in my arms and held her fiercely.

"Darling," she cried. "Don't."

It took me several seconds for her appeal to register. I freed her slowly and sank back into my chair, listless and oppressed.

I do not want to leave the impression, certainly it would be a false one, that I did nothing but loll in luxurious fashion with my wife. I managed some work of my own, in my study, and I attended to the farm business. This last now took less time. I went to the fields only half as much, which was due in part to my better knowledge of the farm's routine and to what I might expect of the tenants. But most of this extra time came from Johnny's frequent appearance about the house. He seemed to take an interest in our venture and a genuine liking for Ellen. He had managed some way to get her a girl to help in the kitchen and without saying a word added the care of the apartment to that of the study. Seeing him more frequently allowed me to dispose of details of farm business which ordinarily would have taken me out.

One evening about milking time he came up to tell
me the cows had got out. There were few fences on the
place. I had not been able to get wire or posts; we had
done the best we could with patching up, but good eat-
ers, and they always make good milkers, will push
through an old fence to greener stuff on the other side.
The tale he had to tell was of an irate neighbor. The
man, a Swede, and amiable enough himself but domi-
nated by a wife who stood very much on her rights, had
found the cows in his alfalfa. It was time to milk and
the Swede had impounded the herd. Johnny suspected
the Swede's wife had her eye on the extra milk, so nothing would do but I must go and free our stock.

In my haste I was well into the yard before I discovered I had forgotten my hat. Johnny glanced politely
but significantly at my head. I at once turned around
and, thinking fast, remembered I had left it on a chair
in my office. It is a peculiarity of mine to dislike hats,
an oddity which goes unnoticed in the opportunism of
urban life. In the country, however, for a man of my
station to go about the place uncovered, which I frequently did, made me seem odd enough to my neighbors,
almost an outlander, at the least a man of eccentric
habits and therefore of doubtful consequence. To go
abroad in such a state of undress, on so formal and
delicate a matter, would have put me in a highly dis-
advantageous position for the business which pressed
for settlement.

So I hurried upstairs to the study. How little a man
knows what he will find when he seeks. The moment I

stepped into the room I felt a change come over it, a sudden drop, as if all the air had fled out of it. I was the only solid thing left, as heavy as marble and gross as lead, the center of a vacuum into which, on the instant, a stillness rushed, impalpable, impenetrable, and charged with the threat of an unnamable evil. The evil was not long in defining itself. How I knew it, or when it became clear, I cannot say, but I felt I was being watched by unseen eyes. I felt what all feel who suffer such exposure, the terrible compulsion to confront it. I knew exactly, with the sixth sense which warns, the direction of the intrusion: the north window above the outside stairway. I stood in a direct line of its view. Between me and it stood a desk. Casually I strolled forward and cunningly pretended to search among the papers which littered the desk's top; and then slowly, without moving my head, I raised my eyes. I brought them up until they reached the height at which I thought to find whatever I had to meet. I met nothing but an uninterrupted view of the encroaching dusk. At eye level the window lights were as transparent as glass can be.

But yet I was not freed. The same pull of that mysterious tension, fluid as water, strong as gut, drew my eyes yet upward. And there at the very top of the window, just out from the edge of one of the blinds which had blown to, I saw a face. It pressed against the pane in passionate anguish, its nose crushed white and its eyes, as limpid as a hawk's and dark as sin, leveled upon mine. I did not waver. I gave it back as straight a stare as it gave me. And then into my stare it vanished. It was there: it was not there, so sudden do these intruders complete their visitations. But it lasted the strokes my heart beat out the world's dark rhythm, an interval long enough for me to know all I had to know. Although the evening was rapidly falling, I saw as brightly as in a vision, with an unimpeachable certainty, that the face belonged to the visitor I had first met in the gallery's arch. But the horrible discovery, which attested to the rapid advance in our relationship lay just in the stare he gave me and I gave back. Whatever he sought, whatever his business there, it was not with me. It comes back, as I recount it, with all the immediacy of the actual experience—it comes back in the intimacy I was made to feel with him. When his glance left mine to travel over the room, I was ignored as if I did not exist, or as if I were so deep in his purpose as to be his other self. It was this affront which banished the shock of this second encounter and sent me flying out of the room to overtake him before he could vanish— this and the knowledge that he had come there to do harm. I arrived on the back stairs in less than five seconds, but the stranger was nowhere to be seen.

The stairway made a curve which brought it under the shelter of the kitchen porch. Down the stairs I bounded, but he was gone. I felt no relief at this but anger that a second time he had escaped me. For form's sake I searched the back premises, I remounted the stairs and took a farther view. There were shrubs and outhouses and the old garden wall, behind which he could have hidden, but it came to me in that moment of search that he was not to be found in any such places. I drew out of the deep knowledge of the experience that I was the key to what he sought. I was the door through which he must pass to his loathsome desire. When I understood this, I was possessed of the calm, almost the comfort, which follows the dread of the unknown threat at last brought out and channelized.

Now that I knew my adversary, for it never occurred to me that he could be other than this, I decided to study him. This brought the impulse to see how he had so easily placed himself at the point of vantage to see into the room. The chimney narrowed at the level of the floor. I stepped upon it and with my hand on the blind peered around, just as I had seen him do. I found that my face fell a good foot below the face I had seen, but it evidently was high enough to frighten Johnny, who had at that moment come into the room, no doubt to see what had delayed me. I saw him stop in his tracks as I had stopped, and stare just as I had stared. His face could not pale, but it looked overlaid with a thin film of wood ashes. By that I could measure the degree of his fright. He turned on his heel and fled the room. I got down in time to meet him.

"'Fore God, Mister Brent," he said, "what ails you?"

"What ails all men," I said, enjoying in my grim way the little scene about to be enacted.

"It ain't dat," he came back at me more vigorously than I had ever known him to.

58

"It's not, Johnny?" I returned with just a shade of irony.

"You ain't hongry, and you ain't daid."

"No, I ain't hongry and I ain't dead, but what would you say if I told you I had met, eye to eye, one foot above where you saw my face, pressing against the glass, in pain and in desire, the one thing more drawing than hunger, the only thing as irrevocable as death?"

"Yes, sir," he said, his eyes opened to the yellow balls, and unfocused, like one aroused in the middle of the night.

"Why don't you ask me what it is? Don't you want to know?"

"What it?" he asked gruffly. His voice measured the strength of his emotion, strong enough, and that was strong indeed, to make him forget the amenities.

"Fate," I said.

I could see his relief as his body relaxed. But he was still not quite reassured. He did not know the word, but he thought it might disguise a more homely terror he would be able to recognize. His shoulders leaned slightly forward. "What do hit look like?" he asked.

"What does it look like?" I paused for the pure pleasure of it. "The terror of the deep."

"Yessir, but can you handle it?"

"I will know that perhaps too late."

He thought awhile and then with great dignity, restored to his manners and feeling the security of their limits, he said, "Mr. Brent, please sir, would you name it to me in your own words?"

"You mean, will I make you see it?"

"I don't rightly know as I wants to see hit. I wants to know what you seen."

"The shape of terror?"

"Yes, sir. Is hit big as you?"

"A head taller," I said. "A handsome face but ravished." I saw him nod. "With deep black eyes, a long rangy body, a black round-brimmed hat on his head."

"Yes, sir, yes, sir," he responded eagerly.

"Wearing a coat such as . . . such as preachers wear."

"Yes, sir."

"And in his hands a staff, not that he needs it to walk with . . ."

"Him need air thing to walk with!"

"Then you've seen him?" I cried.

"Seen him? Sho', I've seed him."

"Where? Where?" I could feel my eyes glow with triumph.

"Why, that's Major Brent," he said and then added quietly, "I sees him all the time."

CHAPTER EIGHT

I KNEW that sooner or later I would have to have it out with Johnny. Now that the issue was joined I must secure my rear. I must discover just where Johnny's loyalty lay. I must know what he saw, but more than that, exactly what communication existed between him and the former master of *The Grove*. I come right out with it. I do not speak of ghosts or apparitions, I speak of Major Brent. To give a name to evil, if it does nothing else, limits its range and that is the beginning of accepting it. A week passed before an opportunity presented itself, the last week, as I remember, of July. Johnny had come up to tell me the corn and the tobacco had been worked over and to find what orders I had to give. We were in my study. I had him sit down in the chair opposite my desk. As I opened the conversation I was surprised at the calm, matter-of-fact tone I assumed. I might have been a doctor inquiring into the nature of a disease. "You must tell me, Johnny," I said, "just what you see—and how often."

He said rather too quickly, "I don't see nothen no more."

I could tell he had foreseen this conference and had

come with his answers ready. Of course I could not let it rest there, although I had already learned by his manner to me, a greater deference, one thing I wanted to know; the company I now kept, so he thought, gave me a status which assured me I should fear no treachery from within the citadel. But this was not quite all I wanted to know, so I continued, "At what times has this visitor to *The Grove* appeared to you?"

He did not answer at once, but my eyes bored into him and held him locked in their vice. How shall I describe my feeling of power at this moment except to say I felt ageless? I held him until at last he spoke as one speaks out of sleep, his words bursting in a volley. "In de full of the moon."

"Always so?"

He nodded carefully. "Just befo'e d' moon change."

"Ah," I breathed, and then like a pistol shot, "but where?"

"Where ere he a mind to."

"But where in particular?" I insisted.

He thought awhile, then said, "Sometime he walk de fields, or sashay in and out'n the trees at the aidge of the woods."

I put my arms on the desk and leaned forward. "Did you ever see him inside the house?"

Cautiously he shook his head.

"But never to have seen him is no reason to believe he doesn't go there?"

"He know the way," he said.

"Does he ever speak?"

He shook his head again, then after a silence which seemed an emptiness rather than a break in time, he whispered, "He ain't need to."

"You mean?" I prompted.

"I knows what make him walk."

"Yes?"

"He doan rest easy."

"And why doesn't he rest easy?"

"All the meanness he done plague him."

"Johnny, were you ever scared?"

"No more'n to make me step light. I knowed I ain't done him no harm. I be layen in bed and tereckly I see he shadow flicker on the wall. 'Thar he,' I say. 'I must git up. He might need sumpum.' Sally Betts draw the quilts over her haid, but I gits up and pulls my clothes on. He'll go plunderen around and me followen."

Johnny stopped talking as if he had said all there was to say. But I had not heard all. So I asked, "What does he look like he's after?"

"He look powerful sad. He look lak he druv the world away and tryen to git it back with a lump of sugar."

"But what is it really, do you think, he is trying to get?"

"He know," Johnny said abruptly.

And that was all I could get out of him. When he left, I noted more particularly the niceness of his manner to me: it was the respect for and the deference to one who engages himself against impossible odds. This was of course easily explained by the superstitions of all simple people. He as well left me assured on another point. I had been fairly certain that Johnny saw no more than all those who believe in ghosts see, that is, the shadow of their imaginations, filled by old stories, myths which grow like moss about the ruin of the cornerstone.

But this was not what *I* saw. What I saw, I saw alone. I could in no way be complicated by my naïve attendant. And yet it was clear he would be of use to me, for I must have some relief from my unbearable knowledge, and he could serve in just this. To shut up my mind, never to talk, would drive me beyond my strength. Ellen I could not approach. So on this, for the time, we parted, I having got from him what I wanted and he—well, I must have seemed a proprietor of a very singular property, whose lines held matter for perilous argument.

CHAPTER NINE

*M*ORE and more I felt the need to know the particulars of Major Brent's past. It was not straining credulity to assign to him more than an ordinary life. However, I needed some clue, and this I knew I could get from Johnny. He had hinted at things. I wanted to bring out to the light, or to the darkness, of my predicament what lay concealed in his mind. At the first opportunity I cornered him. "What," I asked, "did you mean when you told me you knew what made Major Brent walk?" He returned my stare, the only movement in his face the cloudy film which closed over his eyes, hiding his humanity behind the mask he presented me. And so he stood and so I let him stand, in the sure knowledge that he would speak in the end, despite the mask, despite the depths of his natural and supernatural caution. I had advanced very deeply in our relationship, for the magic of words had at last put him at my disposal.

"I done tole you all I knows," he said.

I knew this was the beginning of more, so I continued, to give him the momentum he needed. "Major Brent has singled me out, and I must find why. I have not turned aside, nor will I. This he suspects and it is for this he hates, perhaps fears, me. Whatever his power in the place he inhabits, in this world he is as helpless as my shadow, unless I make some blunder and through carelessness give him the substance he lacks. Now that you have spoken of him to me—" I said this slowly with great solemnity—"him you will never see again." I turned abruptly. "What does he lack that he disturbs my peace?"

Johnny remained as motionless as some black idol, with the thick hands bent to the curve of work lying blocked out in his lap, but at last he began to talk. The words passing his beefy lips came simply and with compassion and with the vast relief of one who disburdens himself of a secret too dangerous to keep or to tell, except to the muted ears of a culprit about to mount the scaffold, where all must be anonymous. In some such fashion, I felt, he considered me.

"The old folks say he always hongry. Hongry befo'e he eat and hongry after he wipe he mouf and belch. He wo'e six women out and made husks of his chillurn. The boys was windbroke before they knowed what he done to'm. When the hands taken out the mules, they'd drap in the lot, too tared to wallow. And the boys 'ud drap, too tared to eat. But they never studied not minden him, and he kept tellen them, if they wanted him to give 'em anything, to hold fast to the plow." Johnny paused and looked beyond me, then: "Nair one of 'm taken time out to marry except the youngest and he pa drove him onto the big road. The boys wrinkled up, but the Major clicked his heels in the air."

"Yes," I said. "What about the daughters?"

"Miss Euphemy. She war his onliest gal. He never give her away. Couldn't find nobody good enough to suit him."

Johnny lifted one hand and lay it heavily over the other and seemed to fall into a doze, but I brought him out of this subterfuge. "There is something you are keeping back," I said. "And Miss Euphemia?"

"They say she taken to locken him in his room." He indicated my study as the place.

"Why?" I was like an inquisitor.

"That ain't for me to say."

I received this rebuke in silence, which I tried to make as ominous as possible, and then Johnny cast his eyes down and said slowly, reverently, and no louder than a whisper, "One day Miss Euphemy called the boys to the house and said they pa was too feeble to walk. They must carry him to the fields. They lifted him in his cheer, with two poles run through it, and him setten up in the air dressed like a bridegroom. Them boys was already blowed from the day's work, but he had 'm tote him through ever' last field on the place. It was sundown when they come to the barley field." He hesitated, as if to recollect the exact details of the scene and then resumed. "He made them boys put postes in the ground and heist him on top of 'm. They swayed on their feets they was so weary, but he didn't offer to let 'm set down. He never said nothen for a spell, but just set there and looked around. It was a turrible fine year for grain. Except for the tobacco the whole place **from** line to line

67

was yaller with barley and wheat and oats. And him jest setten there looken at hit, until the boys and the hands circlen around got nervious, for the sun was nigh to drappen.

" 'Hit's purty and hit's mine,' he say. 'Hit's the purtiest crop I ever seen at *The Grove* and the biggest yield.' My pa heared him say them words. Then he stood up and taken one look around and dropped in his cheer. The postes rocked, but didn't nobody come nigh to sturdy 'm. It was gitten along towards dark before he roused hese'f again. 'Hit's taken me my life to do this,' he said. '*The Grove* has done the mostest hit can ever do. I knowed they was a perfect crop in it. Look around you and see it, for you'll never see air other one.' The boys looked about 'm foolishlike, not knowing what the old man had in mind. But he warn't long in naming hit. He reached in his big pocket and pulled out a sack. 'Lemuel,' he called. 'Sir,' his son answered like a boy and him in his fifties. He pitched him the sack and Lemuel caught it. 'Amos,' he said, and Amos stepped forward. He pitched him a sack. And then he called Josh and Abner and pitched them a sack. 'I'm given you each a thousand dollars in gold for your hire. It will start you in the world, for this place you will never till again. It has reached perfection. It can do no more.' He come to a stop and nobody didn't know what to say, but he spoke up once more and for the last time. 'I want ever' stalk of grain to fall where it grows and ever hill of tobacco to rot where it stands. My everlasting displeasure to him that tries to reap what I sowed. Now you may take your pay and go.'"

Johnny's voice stopped.

"And . . ." I said.

"My pa said the hands slipped away and nair one looked back. And the boys stood around like chillurn who'd lost their way, and then they left. And my pa said he never seen sich a bright light on no old man's face. He looked like a body busten out of the creek all wet with glory. Then it come to Pa he war the last one there. He had to pull his feets out of the ground to run. He said he shet his eyes and run, and when he opened 'm again the dark had growed out'n the fields and swallowed up the house. He shuck all night, afeared for day to break. He knowed them fields 'ud be bare as he hand."

"And were they?"

"Naw, sir. The fields was yellow as butter."

"And Major Brent?"

Johnny shook his head. "The cheer sot up 'ar in the air."

"Yes?"

I thought he would never get it out.

"It sot up 'ar, plumb empty. And one crow roosten on hit's back."

CHAPTER TEN

*J*OHNNY had given me the clue I wanted, but only the clue. I knew I would have to untangle it. My imagination whirled on the periphery of my predicament. It was not ready to plunge to the depths of the center of truth. I deliberately refrained from making a premature decision. I drifted, if to circle slowly down the narrowing cone may be called drifting. There was time, but not too much time, to make decisions before the giddy swirl and the plunge and the suck.

The month of August went quietly enough on the surface. It was notable for one thing: the last opportunity for withdrawal. In the most cleverly conceived strategems of doom, whether contrived by man or by supernatural powers, there comes a moment when escape is possible, a moment of clarity when the strain is released by its own tension. The way is always opened up by some incident in the daylight world, as plain, as restricted as a banker's books, and telling as little as do these books about the accounts they record. Though they tell little, without the understatement of such things as the double entry we would submerge ourselves hopelessly in the confusion of the multiple depths

70

of our natures. The orderly life of individuals and society depends on the balance between light and darkness. We perish only when the sun gets jammed at high noon or the moon glides forever at the full. The chance to withdraw came to us in an offer for the farm. It was as plain and direct as that. A mild land boom brought a buyer to our remote location. He offered me a modest profit over and above all that I had put into *The Grove*. I took this offer to Ellen.

I found her in the kitchen. Tired of waiting for me to help, she had begun doing it over herself. Some way she had got together several girls of the neighborhood and they were painting the walls. She stepped down at my request from a stool, flushed from her work. A dash of paint spotted her cheek like a beauty spot. A strand of hair had got loose and lay fetchingly over her forehead. I saw her, as sometimes happens, with the freshness of our first meeting. This sight of her brought with it as well the state of mind of our courtship, when the world seemed as giving as the demands we would make of it. It was an unhappy vision, for it weakened my resolve to retreat.

We sat on the porch and lighted cigarettes.

"Isn't it going to be lovely?" she asked.

"The kitchen?"

"I've got it all planned. A double sink, shelves on the side, on the north end closets for brooms and things, and if you could only cut me a window . . ."

"Before we do all this, I've something to tell you."

"I know. We haven't the money. But, look, I can

sell this ring. It's a rather nice one. I've got it all fig-
ured out. It will just, with careful planning, do what
I want to do. I'd much rather my kitchen glittered than
my hand. We don't go anywhere any more."

"Darling, I've had an offer for the farm."

"Oh." A pause. "How much?"

"A small profit."

"Oh." Another pause. "If it were a lot of money . . ."

"Of course if we really want to stay here. It's only
a chance to get out without a loss."

"Do you want to leave?" she asked. "I had no idea
such a thought had entered your mind."

I evaded her question. "I only thought I had got you
into something tougher than I knew. I'm offering you
a chance to get out with honor."

"Don't say me, darling. You got *us* into something,
a something I'm rather beginning to like."

"I must point out," I went on, "the tremendous job
still ahead."

She thought for a while. "Well, darling, whatever
you think we ought to do."

"You know how I hate to turn loose, but you've been
rather on my conscience."

"Why should I be on your conscience?" She looked
at me frankly.

Hastily I said, "It's not that altogether. I've doubts
about myself."

"Doubts?"

"Well, I'm not sure I can handle it, that I can, well,
make you happy here."

She got up. We strolled out onto the lawn and sat under one of the large cedars. Elsewhere in the world which is August it was dry. The corn was twisting in the fields, the pastures were dusty, and even at night the cattle lowed with distress. Everywhere the sun beat down in the direct scorching way which only an August sun can do—everywhere except on our lawn. There is little shade to a cedar but there was plenty of walnut and oak to protect the grass. It was hot but there was still green for the eye to rest upon. Ellen leaned back against the trunk of the cedar. I lay on my back before her.

"This is a pleasant place," I said, beguiled by the clarity of the sun and the sanity of the physical world, when it pauses at recess and its real nature goes out of mind. "This *is* a pleasant place," I repeated.

"And it can be a fine place," she added. "I acted rather badly in the beginning," she went on, "but then I was overwhelmed. Now it seems simpler. I am happier. It is better for you than the town. There you always ran on the exhaustion of nerves. Perhaps in time we may have children."

I put my arms about her waist. "You are the only reality," I said. "I don't care if we can't have children. Our life is meaning. Everything else is illusion. Nothing must take you away from me."

Gently she released herself. "Darling, you make me a little afraid. Nothing is going to take me away from you."

And so it was decided to stay on. As we went back

to the house, hand in hand, the intruder seemed no more threatening than a bad dream after breakfast and coffee.

At the door we were met by the mailman. He had a registered letter. I opened and read it.

"What is it?" Ellen asked.

"It's from my nephew Moss," I said. "He's being sent home from the South Pacific. It doesn't say why." I handed her the letter. She glanced through it.

"He is rather brief, isn't he?"

"I hope he is in no trouble," I said.

"You can never tell what the military will do. Probably battle fatigue." And then she said cheerfully, "He can help with the house. It will do him good to do a little honest work."

"Yes, yes," I said. "It will do him good. It will do us all good to see him."

But as I went into the house, I carried with me a strange feeling of foreboding.

CHAPTER ELEVEN

*A*FTER this I felt we lived just as other people do. The false romanticism which had landed me so blithely into the bramblebush of history tempted me with the prospect of success. The actual undertaking as opposed to the idea had impressed on me the heroic nature of the work and, as with all sagas, the involvements with the supernatural. My initial encounters with the shade of Major Brent, or whatever metamorphosis he had assumed, found me possessed of a courage I didn't know I had and an exquisite awareness of horror whose depths sank below and beyond mortal knowledge. The secret awareness that I was no hero I buried. In the same grave I put the fear that my courage was unequal to the perils of my situation. In the blind panic which was my state of mind but which seemed, because of its long duration, a clear, lofty objectivity, I banished Major Brent to his proper habitat and forbade him to trespass again. My first presentiment that all was not right with my nephew Moss faded into the picture of him as my heir, and I longed for his arrival. It seems rather complicated even now, but it all came from my talk with Ellen and her desire to live at *The Grove,* which meant of course that all would be

well with us and my love for her. I don't think that I
understood how my original interest in the place had
shifted its emphasis. I still thought of myself in all sincerity as occupied with the difficult problems of regeneration. Our personal problems I took to be merely a
variant on the central theme. But actually my interest
now lay almost entirely and rather desperately in making *The Grove* seem attractive to Ellen. I was occupied
with the usual American bourgeois habit, in spite of my
ideas, in spite of my very principles, of giving my wife
the comforts, the setting, the status equal to my love for
her. In the beginning, when she went to pieces, the ruin
of our love seemed imminent and my manhood threat-
ened. Now that I see things so clearly I am certain that
a loss of manhood was involved, for had I not caught
from the infested air that disease of all latter-day
Americans—to fail in a material way is to fail in manhood?

In such fashion I allowed myself to be taken off
guard. There are no other words for it. What devious
ways does not an imperfect apprehension take us?
Had I been put on record before a jury of sensible men
—I do not say peers, for where in the sweepings of
this continent could the peer to such extravagant in-
dividualism have been found—and had I been asked in
the presence of the twelve, Can you do it? I at least
would have paused and assessed the odds for what they
were worth, for I am a man of vision. But how we blot
out in the gloom of mad endeavor the light which by
exposing will thwart us!

And so it was, I say again in all honesty, I retired to my study where I worked every day and often far into the night at reviews and essays to get the material for our little campaign. I had had to borrow on the property to add to the sale of Ellen's ring, for it took a great deal to keep her in the frenzy of her work. She handled laborers better than I and, more quickly than I had dreamed, managed to finish the kitchen, the dining room, and get a start on the lower hallway. I worked confidently and scarcely felt the pressure of our economic situation. And yet of course it was money I had on my mind, so much so that I didn't dare think of it, lest I think to what ruin and disaster its lack would bring us.

And money did begin to come in, slowly at first in steady small sums, enough for the household expenses and a little laid by against the interest on the mortgage whose payment drew nearer with each ticking of the clock in the hall below. I raced my mind against the swinging of that round brass sun. It became an obsession with me. There endured such a synchronization between my mind and the clock's stroke that so long as I worked I could not hear it. But let me grow idle, or rest, it struck off with its impervious beat precious time forever lost. I now think I must have been a little mad. I dared not look the timepiece in the face but always hurried by with averted eye; yet I could never go fast enough. Once I thought by ignoring I had silenced it, but it stopped me in the doorway through which I fled. If only once it would miss a beat, but the unvarying regularity of the tick, the swing, and the tock drove me to desperate and inhuman work. Ellen appealed to me, saying I would be ill. Not even she could divert me. I could point to the need and the proofs in the form of the checks I showed her. What I could not point to were the terribly inhuman odds I strove against, and I do not speak of material things, but of those regions where time is unknown.

In no circumstances would I have broached the subject of those regions. The strangest comment on my state of mind was the way I was able to shut it out of my own thoughts. Its return came with the shock almost of a betrayal. I must have been asleep, how long I have no way of knowing, except that it was well after midnight—I had heard the stroke of that hour. My arms lay on the desk. They had disarranged the papers there and from the night sweat several pages of my novel still clung damply to my flesh. All I know is I found myself sitting erect and wide awake in the pressure of that alien and frigid atmosphere I had come to know and dread. My eyes were blurred from too much use of the tight sleep of the overtired, but they were clear enough to see through the open door the loathsome form of my guest. He hovered in the doorway to our apartment and I saw his left hand fumble as if he were trying to find the knob. So still was he, except for the purpose in that hand and arm, swollen to my view out of all proportion to the rest of his form, that I had the sickening illusion of the hypnotic sway of a snake practicing at the keyhole. My alarms and my

78

disgust were equal. These overbore any thought of fear or courage. I was merely drawn to go forward and challenge him.

I arose from the chair and it made a long creaking sound of pain. With this sound in my head I strode onto the gallery and stopped within a few paces of the shadowy figure whose back was still turned to me. But let it not be understood that the figure was in any way vague. The frightful presence could have been no clearer had it been day at its brightest hour. Slowly the hand withdrew from the keyhole and the arm, so easily did it move, floated to his side. By this I knew he had become aware of me and, feeling an exalted elation at this recognition, I waited for his next move. I waited in the alarm of the tremendous advance he had made in the freedom of the house, for only now, at a range so close I could have touched him, did some part of the meaning of his persistence grow clear to me. But I had no leisure to examine it. He had turned.

He had turned to face me. I did not waver nor fall back but, all taut, met him. At once, for there was no mistaking it, I sensed the change in his bearing to me. I was no longer ignored as I had been in that encounter in our study, where his examination of the room in my presence gave me the queer feeling that he took me for an accomplice. There was none of this. It was clear now that he recognized in me the sole obstacle to his desire. I got it all from the hollow depths of his stare. I remember nothing of the features, only his look of hatred and malevolence which somehow included himself as well as me. These are hit-or-miss words. There is nothing in the human catalogue of feeling which I can draw on for analogy. I knew this: his appearance which I already felt too much to bear grew yet more intense. It enveloped the space we stood in, or what became space some moments afterward, for here again I stumble over words. The air, if air it was, made a chill and a silence in which nothing existed. Even I felt no true sense of being. We were isolated in some intermediate world. Not a sound penetrated from the night outside it, where the actual darkness disclosed its imperfections before the true image enveloping me. Though in the world I was shut off from it, or to draw a finer distinction, that part of the world where I was had been usurped by another. The chill was the dry chill of absolute aridity and the silence a silence of endless reaches where no sound was or ever would be.

Then my senses whirled under the impact of metamorphosis. I felt myself shift ground before a blast of heat. Perhaps I cried out, for the sudden contrast of what went before and what came after gave me a moment of pain. When I recovered myself, I saw that I was alone on the gallery, on a sultry August night, with not a breath of air stirring.

CHAPTER TWELVE

I HAD barely got my equilibrium back before I received another shock, coming so hard on the first that the impact of the second seemed only a continuation of the first. It was the revelation of the purpose behind the apparition's return. The shock was the sickening effect this intelligence had on me. It surged through me with the clarity of euphoria—his position at the door to the apartment where Ellen slept, the intention in that ghastly hand. I know now that even at the time of his first appearance I nurtured some such fear, never daring, because of the insupportable implications it contained, to bring it up for candid inspection.

There was no doubt now about its being full blown. I knew, even though I cannot tell you why I knew, that I had prevented some terrific act of violence, some dreadful adventure in which space and matter were involved. I suspected Major Brent as the agent, perhaps out of a devouring need, the self-appointed agent of doom. The word I know has lost in the soilure of too many tongues its meaning. This meaning I now restore. Say the word aloud. Believe you speak it for the first time and you will understand the terror of my comprehension. You will understand my anxiety and reluctance to rush through the door and take Ellen in my arms, for, alas, I am earth-bound and subject to all the laws of matter. To defend what I loved against a force I could never reach—this was the excruciating nature of my torture. Had I even now lost her? Major Brent had vanished, but Ellen? I felt I had been in time, but could I—always this uncertainty—could I be sure? There was but one way to find out. Open the door and go forward into the room. This I did.

Noiselessly the door swung inward and, dark though it was, I could feel myself pale at what I saw: Ellen swaying just inside, in the nightgown she had worn on our wedding night, her eyes open but still asleep. The gown moved lazily against her body, blown by the sultry air which the door in its passage had stirred. She gave a little gasp and stepped back as my hands grasped her. And so we stood for an instant as I tried to speak. What came from my mouth sounded like the cry of an animal in pain. At last I said the useless words, "Darling, what are you doing here?"

She said rather wanly, "I thought I heard you call. I must have been asleep."

Gently, as one is careful of an invalid, I picked her up and laid her upon our bed. As I fumbled at the buttons of my shirt, she said, "Dear I've had the most awful dream."

"Yes, I know," I said. With great care I tried to calm my voice.

"But how can you know?" she asked.

I did not answer. The buttons would not undo.

"Oh," she said and her voice was clearer. "What made you tear your shirt. You've none too many."

I mumbled something about the dark. I could not speak, I could not quiet the great perturbation in my heart until I lay beside her and had her body in my arms. Nothing but this old substantial truth could restore me.

At last I was beside her and she received me. Calmed, I lay on my back in the empty heaviness of release. Only our fingers now entwined. Out of a great distance she said, "I thought you had forgotten."

"Forgotten?" I repeated.

"That this is our anniversary."

I hedged. "How could you think that?"

"You've seemed so . . . well, so absorbed. At times I feel you don't know I'm here."

"You know what I've been doing. How I've had to."

"That's just it. Do you have to be alone all the time?"

I shifted ground. "Aren't you . . ." I hesitated.

"Happy?" she interposed and then her voice trailed off. When she spoke again, she seemed to speak out of some private truth. "Happiness. Oh, I don't know that that matters now."

I pretended to be calm, but what agonizing considerations laid waste my peace of a few moments ago! My voice must have sounded queer to her. It sounded queer enough to me as I said, "Happiness doesn't matter?"

"It's not that it doesn't matter. But there are other things."

"Other things?" My voice was casual, except for a slight tremor.

She turned and said with a kind of puzzled desperation, "I know you've got your writing to do, but, darling, you mustn't leave me alone so much."

"I shall never let you out of my sight again."

"I didn't mean all that, Henry."

"What did you mean then?"

She answered me in her own way, and I felt the pathos of her sad little gallantry, for what once had quieted all needs, answered all questions, had become itself the dark field of ultimate questioning. My head was still whirling with the various possibilities when at last her fingers fell loose from mine and I noticed the first misty smudge of day slide up the gap in the flowered curtains. In this faint light I looked at her pale lovely face, now closed to me in sleep. Had it closed to me forever? Had I, after all, been too late? Did the dissembling mask of sleep contain what I would find when the tale was all told? I probed into my consciousness, but it only gave back the wonder of my anguish and my desperate need. I longed for the future instant by instant, the flash of vision which would reveal my condemnation or my reprieve. I got the knowledge of a duller thing, the unhurried, unvarying lockstep which is time. If to this prison I resigned myself, it was not entirely without hope. Its restraining power restrained also another.

CHAPTER THIRTEEN

I MUST have dropped off, lying at her side, for I found myself sitting up in bed, my heart in a stifled pounding from the sudden wrench to consciousness and the sense that I had missed some terribly important engagement. I saw that I was alone. The curtains were still drawn, but the quality of light shining through the flowered figures told me how much of the morning was already spent. Hard on this came the awareness that while I slept another had had the chance to enjoy the freedom of *The Grove* with that insolent display of familiarity which made me so long to throttle him. My need to do him physical violence was great and my impotence so apparent that, for a moment, my imagination gave body to that density of air which he assumed at the demand of infamous longing.

I threw on my clothes and rushed from the room. The hours I had been sleeping Ellen had been unguarded. What disaster might not come of it, if once he got through to her, I dared not think. She had felt influences. Of this I was sure, but I was equally sure that I had so far saved her an actual encounter.

Once outside, in the gallery which lay between the study and the apartment, I paused an instant to decide which way to go. Never had I as now understood the full terror and meaning of time. To waste even a breath in a false start might be to lose all in the general waste of eternity. Short as it was, my hesitation allowed me to see through the open door to my study that someone was sitting at my desk. I advanced and found my nephew Moss, completely at ease in my chair, after the manner of young men profligate of that one gift they will spend the rest of their lives regretting. "Have you seen Ellen?" I asked. To this day I am unsure what I got as answer, but my ears caught the phrase, "In the flower garden." Intuitively I knew I had the right direction. With no further greeting or welcome, I rushed on.

The garden lay to the rear of my study. There was a stretch of lawn and then the wall. In other days one could have looked down into the garden, but it was so overgrown I did not pause but right off swung down the winding way. I had been inside it once, on my first visit when I came with the idea of buying *The Grove*. Intuitively I understood the temptations it would have for me and afterward stayed away. The degree to which a farm's economy can be brought is best judged by the flower garden. To have it at all is a luxury and evidence of discipline and sound management, for the garden needs attention always when the crops can least spare a hand from the fields. And of course it bespeaks that leisure which is the supreme attainment of civilized habits. I go as far, even, as to say that in the great ages the formal garden reflects the last refinements of

the social pattern and, indeed, is the commentary that
the age makes on itself. For what was Versailles laid
out but to inter the feudality of France? Or what is
any eighteenth-century garden but the very will of
fashion, with its geometrical pattern, the clean little
walks between the low, well-trimmed borders, that su-
perior artifice where even the flowers seem denatural-
ized? But the house defines another truth. If it is old,
it contains the whole tradition. One does not make a
house. A house grows and as it grows binds together
the continuous past. Because I understood this, until
I had house and land well in hand, I knew it were best
to stay away from the place I now approached.

The lock and chain had rusted together about the
gate. But this was no hindrance. The wall had many
gaps, where the brick had fallen into rubbish or had
been robbed for various uses about the farm. Very
quietly I pushed aside a straggly and overgrown box-
bush, stepped over and was inside. For a moment I
forgot why I was there. The garden was not large,
yet it was not small, nor was it exactly as I had remembered it. I had had the image of an old-fashioned garden but not the perfect symmetry I now found. Flowers
and shrubs and weeds were all overgrown in a common
tangle, and luxuriantly overgrown from the extraordi-
nary richness of the ground, but beneath this wilderness
the plan was clear. It had been laid out in a circle, with
a round springhouse upon a mound as its hub. A ser-
pent's head, carved of stone, rose up out of the little
brick house, with jaws widespread and dripping water.

Once the water must have poured, for there was still evidence of the conduit circling the beds, each group of plots increasing in size as they approached the enclosing wall. And just here was the final touch of art. The wall, hexagonal in shape, softened but did not alter the meaning of the design. I stood enthralled and a little dizzy from the impact of the mind able to conceive this, the utter daring, the brilliant imagination, the Satanic pride of it. I saw afresh with what an adversary I had to do and again, when I looked to the resources I had, I very nearly gave in to despair. But no matter what the odds the soldier's response to danger is professional— he acts. I was a kind of soldier: I remembered why I was there. Swiftly I searched the undergrowth. I looked with a sharper eye and what I saw wrenched me for a moment from my obsession. The garden was a dump heap. Rotten tin cans, broken bottles, rags, half a fireback, all littered the place. There were piles of ashes, pocked with bits of charcoal beaten to the surface by countless rains, and a thousand other objects of refuse tossed anywhere about. In the midst of this I saw Ellen.

She was on the ground, in a cool white muslin frock, weeding one of the walkways. She did not see me as her head was bent to her work, and I was careful not to interrupt her. There was about her the air of innocence one thinks of as surrounding the sacrificial victim. Her hair had been brought up on her head, and I admired with the sweet sense of possession the purity of the lines of her neck, bent slightly around and down. Then my heart made that plunge of alarm, the infallible awareness of danger. It was all in the fierce rapidity of her hands and, in spite of the illusion of composure, a too rapt attention to what she did. All around her rose piles of weed and grass, neatly raked for the barrow. My gaze widened, startled at the amount of the garden she had cleaned, obviously more than one morning's work. I dared not reckon the number of hours, else I should have had to ask how she had done it at all. My wonderment grew into a question, Why had she made no mention of this to me?

So I was warned but my comprehension was slow to focus. I found myself, of necessity, returning to her hands. They were my clue. Then as I watched, I saw them quicken as though she felt behind her the shadow of the taskmaster. The tension in her frail body was painful to see, and it all drew to a point in the speed of her fingers. Exquisite, fragile, they drove at the dirt under some dreadful compulsion. I took all this in as I took in the certain knowledge that another watched as well as I. A sodden chill rolled out of the depths of the undergrowth, swirling in its circular track until it caught us up in the logic of its motion. All sounds of the bright morning fell away and, as they perished, so did my apprehension of the alien air I breathed. I was no more conscious of the fearful energy which underlay it than I would be aware, walking down a country lane, of the world revolving in space. The sick feeling

I had had of violation, my helpless estrangement before it, now entirely disappeared. It was as one equal to all occasions that I slowly turned my head until, at last, it came to rest facing the garden's center. I paused to sharpen my will. I paused; then I lifted my eyes, brick by brick, up the slimy springhouse wall.

CHAPTER FOURTEEN

I GOT to the study as soon as I could and that meant, of course, as soon as I could get Ellen out of the garden and safely into the house. I shut the door and leaned against it for support. I had kept up my front in the garden. Only now did I give in to the after-effects of my trial of nerve.

"He has got through to her," I gasped to Moss.

There had always been great sympathy between my nephew and me, but never did it show to better purpose than in this, my tacit appeal for help. He confused me by no stupid response, no tiresome questions. He merely leaned forward in his chair and waited for more. The mere sight of him, the wonderful feeling that I would no longer stand alone, this knowledge and the privacy of my room, restored somewhat my equilibrium. I had retired to my citadel and my faithful seneschal was at my side; or to draw a sharper figure, my heir.

So it came about that what I had to divulge was given and received as a matter of family concern. It was the ease and grace of his reception that gave me the firm ground I needed, the familiar rapport which usually passes between father and son. Whatever the virtues of Moss Senior, and he was reputed to have many in certain circles, they did not thrive in his dealings with his son. My brother lived in the happily simple world where all things have a price, and the better the bargain the better the price, which is all very well, I suppose, if you don't drive bargains for the affection of your son. I never thought I would have sympathy for such limitations, but I fairly blessed them now as I quickly sketched for Moss the history of what had happened up to his appearance at *The Grove*. The boy's reception of my tale was so keen and ready it gave me the illusion of talking aloud to myself. "And so you see," I wound up, "I have failed, miserably failed."

"Failed?" I rather felt than heard the question, so softly did it drift my way.

"Yes, failed. To stand between Major Brent and his odious purpose."

"What is . . ."

"What is his purpose? It is also his desire." I fairly spat these out, so fresh was his fearsome image in my mind.

"And that?"

"I don't quite know. Oh, that I did!" I finished with a groan of perplexity. "I do know that it has to do with Ellen. Of this I am certain as I am certain of you, there, in my chair."

"How do you know?"

"How? How? I saw."

The shadow of a question crossed my nephew's

eyes. It was plain I needed to be more circumstantial.
"Not an hour ago, there in the garden, I beheld him
with my eyes, like an evil smoke but also a solid, hovering above the springhouse. He filled my eyes and
then went, like mist drying, down through the rotten
floor."

"Did . . ."

"Did Ellen see? No, but she felt. She knew he was
there."

"How?"

"I could tell by the look on his devilish face."

"But if she didn't see?"

"But I saw. The eager gleam, the contaminating
look of his triumph." And I added in a low voice, at
the marvel of it, "And it reached out like a solid thing
and touched her. It was then I could stand no more.
He disappeared." At the thought of this I fell silent,
trembling before the memory of this hateful appearance. And as I looked across at Moss, I could see
that it had welled up into my eyes by the reflection
from his. More smoothly, for hatred is like hardening a stick by fire, I developed the line of my reason-
ing. "I had thought I stood between—he will not
hold up to me, you see, he has his limitations too—
but what I learned today is that some traffic has existed between them and for longer than I can know.
What she did, what she was, in the garden showed
me. And I have other cause to believe . . ."

"You mean?"

"We had a chance to sell the farm. She demurred,

after having pleaded to get away. Now what could make her change her mind so suddenly?"

And then I heard, "But how can he get at her?"

"By making her want to come to him."

"But how? An apparition to a mortal being."

"It is one of the oldest stories. And who knows what promises he makes over the invisible lines of his communication—enough," I added grimly, "to make her want to know more."

"Then if she wants to know more . . ."

"His spell is not quite wound up? Good!" I almost shouted. "That may be our way out. We must hold to that. If we can prevent another meeting . . . We must watch, you and I, every hour of the day and night."

"I will watch at night," I heard.

"And I by day." This gleam of hope brought me up sharp to the practical way of carrying out our plan. I asked, "Does Ellen know you are here?"

He shook his head slowly and, for a moment, his eyes seemed to withdraw. With uncanny intuition I understood that he did not want her, or anyone, to know he was here. This brought me up to his own mysterious situation. His cryptic letter and then, without warning, his arrival. I looked more closely, berating myself for a too great preoccupation with my own affairs, and saw his travel-stained uniform, the dust and grime of the battlefield still on it, the pale look of strain and the jagged scar on his forehead running back into his head. I could not tell how far because of the blackness and the thickness of his hair.

I saw at once how painful any questions of mine would be. Matter-of-factly I took it up where he had left off. "I will put you in the old office out there in the yard. Johnny will bring your food. No one—" I emphasized this—"no one need know you are here. It is better that way."

On this we parted. I arose for my watch. It was understood that he would keep the study until night, when his would begin.

CHAPTER FIFTEEN

*A*LL blessings are mixed. So I felt when I had the leisure to think how the tension would slacken now that Moss had come. But this very letting up gave me time to think, and for the first few days my thoughts were equally divided between my wife and nephew. I cannot tell what a wonderful comfort he was unless I also tell what marred this comfort. If I had let myself go, I should have gone as far as alarm at his ambiguous appearance, his noncommittal silence about why he was here and not with his outfit. I gave him every chance to explain himself. I hinted at battle fatigue, at a well-deserved leave. I even went so far as to open a discussion of psychiatry as practiced officially by the Army, saying what an advance it had made over the old brutal methods which reduced human performance to the extremes of cowardice and bravery. But no matter how subtly I threw out these different leads not one of them did he take. He would smile, he would listen politely, he would make some general observation—nothing more. I was forced to come back to my original impression: he was hiding at *The Grove,* but whether because of something he had done or something he feared might be done to him, I had to leave undecided.

This I was willing to do. After all he was here, I needed him, I felt surer somehow of withstanding what there was to withstand, in spite of the rapid and perilous advance of danger, which I never let out of my mind for a moment. It lay with me like a cold spring at the bottom of a pool. On the surface all was warm and even languid, but one had only to dive to know the shock of the chill beneath. I suppose I would have cracked up but for the respite I got from floating in the lukewarm upper surface. It seemed that every-body at *The Grove* conspired to keep me at ease, Ellen, Moss, and Johnny. I was touched at the way Johnny tried to rise to the occasion. When I told him the new duties I entrusted to him, he accepted them with under-standing. He cleaned out the office and set up a bed, pretending he needed it for a storehouse. But the most remarkable instance of his tact showed itself in the way he met Moss. I had brought Johnny up to the study, first warning him that no one must know that my nephew was there. I told him that only he and I knew it, that even Miss Ellen did not know, and that if by any chance it got out, I would know who had been indiscreet. I made no open threat, of course, but my manner was as grave and ominous as I could make it. This, I knew, would leave its impression, for Johnny had conceived a tremendous respect for the possibili-ties of my nature. Moss was standing by the book-case, reading the titles there. I said, "Lad, this is

Johnny. He will look after your needs." Johnny gave
a quick glance to the corner where Moss was, stiffened
slightly—only I would have noticed it—and then stood
there with respectful dignity, hat in hand, looking not
at but just to the side of Moss's position. In any other
situation I would have smiled at his cunning. Nobody
could trap him into admission of seeing anything,
and yet his stance told me he was aware of everything.

Moss turned, smiled in his charming way, and
nodded; then he went back to the books. I never saw
a more difficult situation handled by both parties with
greater ease or discretion. My affection for them increased enormously and it became the seal to our common aim. It led me, without more ado, to probe farther
into the last days of Major Brent on earth. Johnny
had told me much, but there were gaps in the information and there was, as always, the confusing veil
of legend. This I must strip away. "Monstrous on
earth as in the void he inhabits," I began by way of
soliloquy, for speaking the word often leads to truth
which escapes the silent inquiry. Johnny heard but
did not understand. Moss showed by his attention, a
deeper stillness, that he listened. "For was it not monstrous in him to make such an end," I went on, "dis-
possessing his inheritors and bringing his daughter
barren to her shroud, and for himself committing or
permitting that last affront to tradition, the unmarked
grave. Does anyone know where he lies?"

I put this to Johnny direct. I waited in the hiatus

my question made and watched the bare shake of his head. "Ain't no grave."

"But he didn't just lie out like a heathen and let the crows pick his bones. Whatever his wish, whatever his need, he died in a Christian land."

"Yessir," Johnny solemnly said, "I knows of some Christians over towards Oak Grove."

"The authorities would not permit it. There must be the record. The record is the state's evidence of self-perpetuation, the link between the past and the future." I paused to change the tone of voice. "There was bound to be investigation."

I waited again. Johnny cast his eyes before him, covertly in the direction of Moss, showing his reluctance to talk about Major Brent in the presence of any witness, no matter how well recommended he came. But finally he said, "The High Sheriff knocked at Miss Euphemy's do'."

"Ah, hah. That's what I have been waiting to hear."

"And she come to de do'."

"Yes?"

"But hit taken right smart rappen on de do' to bring her. The High Sheriff nigh wo'e out his hat fanning. She opened de do' wide and shaded her eyes . . . so." Johnny lifted the stiff black fingers to his forehead and squinted as one might do who looks into smoke. "She looked over the High Sheriff's lef' shoulder, she looked past his face, she looked over his right shoulder, and then she shet the do'."

That, as far as I could gather, marked the extent

to which the law ever went in attempting to implicate Miss Euphemia. The law must show cause and motive. The keepers of the peace must have felt that there was in Major Brent's act a threat to the general peace. But what had they to go on? An old man, by his own will, drives his sons away and, again by his own will, with witnesses to the fact, remains alone in the middle of his fields. And is never seen more. His very act was a symbol of social violence, but you can't bring a symbol into court. And deeding the land to Miss Euphemia was further proof of his intention, but the deed had been on record a year before his disappearance. All was regular. The proper heirs had no recourse, no expectation of aid from the authorities. They inherited a title, the Dispossessed, and nothing more but a hireling's pay. There would have been much whispering, many dark allusions to the barren woman who lived on at *The Grove,* who gave the name reality by letting the sassafras sprouts take the fields, but the real terror before which the keepers of the peace drew back lay in the meaning of the act itself. And this they had no way of dealing with.

For what can the public guardians do but harden their souls and dance mincingly on the sharp blades of power? And at last fall and eunuch themselves, for the strongest heads grow giddy at last? And clean up the blood of the victim to make ready the altar for the next, for the victim they can neither commit nor save, led all decked in garlands and white, like innocence coming up for confirmation, but coming up to sacrifice

100

and spilt blood to lay the oldest ghost of all, who will not lie but, like the absent lord, returns with the season to collect his dues? Pistol strapped to the bulging side, the ready grin on the florid face, the toothpick after meat, always they find themselves caught in the same dilemma. They hail the fornicator into court, but bastards drool on the doorsteps. They jail thieves, but the honor of the state is compromised by those who deal in its goods. Assaulters they fine, but broken heads mock them each Saturday night. If matters committed to their care, all actions plain to pragmatic eyes, go unresolved for all their resolutions and unchained for all their chains, what then could the High Sheriff do but cool his heels before the fact of a shut door which was not a fact at all but a threat and a symbol as old as night?

"And where will it bring me," I said aloud, "this cold scent, but where all false trails lead—back upon myself?"

"Ain't it the truf?" Johnny agreed and nodded wisely.

And it was the truth and on this I dismissed Johnny who, as so often before, had put it squarely up to me, without incriminating himself.

CHAPTER SIXTEEN

I DIDN'T let out, even to Moss, how hopeless I felt about poor Ellen. So long as I didn't put it into words, I could keep my courage up. Words have a way of fixing a thing and, once spoken, may not be taken back. But the scene I had happened on in the garden was too depressing, even, for courage. As I turned to the springhouse to meet what I had to meet, I gave my back to Ellen. The moment of release I whirled about and met . . . well, I met her eyes. A faint flush brushed her features which had been so pale when I first came into the garden. The strain was all gone, her hands hung limp above the work she had been doing, but it was the eyes which confessed so clearly my fears. There was no avoiding the truth of their stare: they had seen all I had seen and more.

I went to her and lifted her to her feet. If then she had confessed openly and frankly, if she had told me even something of her peril, I might have been able to save her. It was the moment for confidences, and for a fraction of the moment I thought she would throw herself into my arms and ask for aid. But the moment passed. She said instead with an engaging smile—

102

what a brave effort at subterfuge it was—"My, you startled me."

"I noticed," I replied, "your absorption."

She said with strange self-confidence, "This was a place I didn't expect to see you."

"And so you thought you were safe in slipping away."

"Yes."

"And now I've spoiled it all."

"Yes, you have spoiled it all."

The very boldness of this took my breath away. If only she had spoken with brutal intent instead of after the old usage of husband and wife which, because of its falseness, seemed to me all the more terrifying! As she saw my confusion, she went on, she even tried gaiety. "You see, I was not yet ready for the grand surprise."

I could only blurt out, "It was surprise enough."

"Don't you think I'm smart?"

"I have another word for it."

Something in my tone caught her up, for she said quickly, "I mean, haven't I done a lot? And without you suspecting a thing."

"I haven't been completely blind, you know."

"But you haven't known?"

"Known?"

"I mean about the garden. What's been going on here."

It was out between us now, in spite of the deliberate ambiguity of language. If I could only have torn away this last veil and heard the desperate truth, desperately spoken! It was on my tongue to say, "You think you have deceived me? But I know whom you meet and what he wants." But some feeling of caution held me back. I said instead, "Now, Ellen, this is too much." I waved my hand toward the walkways. "I'll send Johnny here to finish up. His crops are about laid by and the boys can help. I want you to stay closer to the house. I can watch you there."

"Watch me, darling?"

"Yes, see what you do." I thought I had carried the game a little far, so I added, "I need to have you near. Besides, this work is too hard for you." I picked up one of her hands. "It will ruin these. That would be a great loss to us both."

Carefully she withdrew her hand. "You should have thought of that when you asked me to come here," she said.

On the way back to the house she stopped once and said fiercely or so I was made to feel the passion in her utterance, "We have got to finish up. I have so little time."

"Time? Time for what?"

She did not answer me, but again I had that feeling of a confidence about to be made and looked my willingness to hear, to help, but she blushed and dropped her eyes and we went the rest of the way in silence.

In the following days I was with Ellen so constantly that what the garden had shown faded out of my consciousness, as the prints of a photographer's proofs fade in the sun. And there was a great deal of sun, which made us think of picnics. The work downstairs had gone so well that Ellen felt we could relax occasionally. She would fix us lunches and we would take to the woods and spread a cloth and eat and talk. It was great pretense and fun. Once we went several miles away, off our land, to a nice creek we knew, and here we spent the day swimming and lying about in the sun. My spirits soared, I even hoped, and if my conscience hurt me, it was on account of Moss to whom I owed such pleasant days and dreamless nights. Once in a mood of confidence I almost slipped up and told her what guest we had in the house. "I have something to tell you, Ellen," I said. "You must try to understand."

"What, darling, have you been keeping back? You've not got some horrible woman tucked away on the back side of the farm, with Johnny standing guard. Johnny has been very mysterious lately."

I caught myself up quickly enough. I took her hand. "No," I said. "It's just that I never really told you how much I love you."

"Will you love me when I'm old and a hag?"

"I'll love you always, no matter what."

"No matter what at all?"

"No matter what at all." I found I had grown suddenly grave.

"That's a large order, you know," she said slowly.

"As long as you want my love, and even when you don't."

"I shall always want it," she said, "and I am trying, you don't know how hard, to make you a good wife." Her eyes blurred and she dropped them, and her voice was low as she said, "But it is hard sometimes. There are things . . ."

"Things?" I prompted.

She leaned across the leavings of our lunch and kissed me. "If it could always be like this . . . if we could stay always this close together . . . if, if this were life and life not what it is . . ."

"Once we thought . . ."

"Yes, I know we thought that food and drink were a bore, something to fill out the interludes between love, that a house was a shelter, and that if we only followed the sun, we wouldn't need that." She turned to me a little sadly. "I remember, you see. It is you who have forgotten."

We were standing now. The sun flared with the false brilliance which dies into dusk and it fell on the littered cloth at our feet. For a moment the reflection from the white cloth, falling across her body, made glary stains on her tan, and then it dazzled my eyes and I closed them. And out of the darkness I said, "No, I haven't forgotten. I've tried to make it stick, forgetting that the honeyed moon passes into leaner quarters and, as a man must who would hold his love, turn the shelter into a house. But when the house is another man's house, and you no proper heir, in spite of title deeds and nine-tenths of the law, you are no better than a guest."

"I'm no guest," she said defiantly.

"No," I replied, and there was all the sadness of our predicament in my voice as I said it, "you are no guest at *The Grove*."

CHAPTER SEVENTEEN

"*F*OR her to say," I repeated to Moss as soon as I could get hold of him, "that she was no guest at *The Grove* brings us straight back to the garden. If she is at home here, and I am not . . . if she is mistress here . . ."

"Well, you are master."

"This is no time for levity," I said rather irritably. "If not you, who then is?"

I paused at the directness of this. There is nothing like the question direct to clear away the vagaries of loose thinking. I rather blushed at what I had been thinking: unconsciously I had accepted Johnny's superstitious belief that Major Brent was master. How absurd this was Moss's plain speaking had made me see, for who can believe in a private resurrection? The dead might return in its own proper air, but no man in his right wits could say that this air could take on body. I had, in truth, come to accept Major Brent without being able to define him. This had confused me. Had he not abandoned *The Grove* to sterility, to a withering up of the traditional vine? Did he not will it to die with him? Then why should I have ever thought that he longed for resurrection? For if my

108

problem was regeneration, his could only be a rising up
to judgment.

"If not you, who then?" The question repeated itself.

I replied out of my bemusement. "Perhaps no one."

"No one?"

I was made to feel a distinctly youthful tone in this.
It might have been my own youth accusing me of the
failure of middle years. I was faced with what all
face who try to explain the complexities of human
experience to the young. I compromised as one does.
I fell back on the logic of the situation. "Major Brent
resents my presence here. You know his history. He
returns out of a jealousy carried beyond the grave.
Don't ask me yet why a shade can feel jealousy."

"But it is Ellen he haunts. Not you."

"And why not? Woman is the carrier of tradition.
His own daughter he kept barren. If he could draw
Ellen to him . . ."

"But how?"

"By luring her to her death," I said abruptly. "Why
else do we keep such strict watch?"

"Is it for this we keep watch?"

"For what else?"

He said casually, "But death is such a common
thing."

There comes a time in all strain when the recoil and
the blow seem but parts of the same movement. At
first I could think no farther than the utter irrelevance
of his remark. I had received him back as the boy I

had known, the dearly beloved nephew who had always looked to me for guidance. I had forgotten the scalding pot of war into which he had plunged. And indeed he had a scalded look, the lacquerlike cast to the features I have sometimes seen on the face of the young who suffer too quickly and violently the ills of the world. In peacetime it is bad enough, the mark of the sophisticate, but in war it is far more sinister, the rushing of experience over knowledge, a surface hardening and all soft confusion beneath. Sadly, as I regarded Moss, I understood that he was a casualty of war, one of those forbidden maturity, the process of curing which allows for the gradual mellowing of the sensibility. The truth was now plain. He had been cast out like spoiled meat.

And I had made him my main dependence. This unexpected complication compromised my whole strategy of defense, but for the moment I could only hedge. I said softly, as one speaks to an invalid, "Don't you think that's beside the point?"

But he looked at me out of his melancholy eyes and shook his head in a slow puzzled way. "It's everywhere, all the time," he said quietly.

"Yes, I know, but . . ."

"I had a friend. We were in the same hole. The water was up to our armpits. I looked away and when I looked back, I saw his head sinking into the water. I lifted him as well as I could. He was there but he was not there. I got no relief for sixteen hours. I just sat in the water with whatever it was left I sat with. It

110

took up as much room as he did, but it wasn't him. I was life, but he wasn't even death. Death was the air which cut across the top of the hole. I knew I had only to lift my head a few inches to find it."

"That was a terrible shock," I said.

"I had another friend," he went on, ignoring me. "He was in my platoon. The platoon was stretched out with good intervals between the men. It had been quiet for some time. It was a quiet sector. We were talking up and down the line. He was some twenty yards away. He called down to me, 'Remember . . .' then a shell dropped. I was knocked out by the concussion and when I came to, all covered with dirt and the smell, I saw a big hole where he had been. I called out his name before I could think. But he wasn't there. He wasn't anywhere. Just that big hole where he had been. I felt a little sick." He paused. "I didn't make any more friends."

"Look, lad, I know," I said, "but . . ."

"No," he replied in the same even voice, "you don't know. But I know. There was so much of it. It was everywhere, all the time."

"That was war," I said. "This is a different thing."

"No," he persisted. "It's no different. What's different is crowding yourself in a hole. You are there and you wait for it, and it doesn't come. You just wait and you think of everything you can think of. You'd be surprised how little there is to think of. It's like a long-drawn-out life where nothing ever happens. The things that bite and crawl and suck keep you alive.

Then it's over." He stopped, but added, "There's one other thing. To love very hard and don't ever do anything but love. As long as that lasts you are alive. Get away from anything that will interfere. Run if you have to."

"You mean I should run away from here?"

He nodded. "There's nothing else to do."

"I can do three things," I said. "I can tell Ellen what I know."

"But you haven't."

"I don't dare. Suppose she's deep in the business."

"So much the better. Before she goes deeper."

"It might drive her all the way."

"Go away."

"That's my second possibility."

"Then go, and now."

"It's not so simple. There is the money tied up here. It's not easy to cut such strings. Nor does any man like to give up."

"Giving up, winning, it's all the same."

"Where would we go now? Even if we could drop what we are doing. Isn't the pillar cut from the same tree as the post?"

"Go away," he said dreamily, "and take your bride away."

"Ellen," I said dryly, "is no longer a bride."

"My love would be always a bride."

"Lying in the slop of foreign holes has addled your wits, son. Listen. Do you think I don't know what a bride is? She is the one with the eyes in the back of her head, seeing both ways at once, the one miracle life is capable of, where innocence and knowledge meet before they fuse in the waste of the world. And you who fancy yourself the perennial bridegroom. Do you think I don't know what he is, at least in this country where there is only one season? He is the man with the strained neck, looking always back to Eden. He tries one way or another, and each time ends up in the blind alley of adultery. Or California."

I had tried to shock a little sense into him, and for a while I thought I had, but he only said, "And the third thing?"

"Stay and see it out."

As he made no comment on this, I filled the silence with my voice. "And that's what I mean to do. See it out."

But the silence remained.

CHAPTER EIGHTEEN

*A*S SOON as I was alone, I got the full impact of the one-two of this blow. Moss could never feel, I now saw, the responsibility for *The Grove* that I had once hoped from him. He would never preserve and hand it on with care to *his* heir. To live for the moment, to burn life up in one great blaze, destroys the traditional thing. His attitude, really, approached much closer to Major Brent's than to mine. Each in his way would sacrifice *The Grove* to the private whim, the personal need of the individual. My disappointment was grave, but it was by no means, at this moment, my first concern. Moss's attitude toward death, which I had learned too late, meant that he would be of no further aid to me. How much of a hindrance I had still to learn. I felt, with some misgivings, that he would not intentionally betray me, but I could no longer put any confidence in him. Nor could I dismiss him easily. He knew too much. There was no way of getting around it. I had added to my burden—I had two now to watch instead of one.

But the first watch was in the hall below, where Ellen was busy taking off the old wallpaper with the help of one of Johnny's girls. I had bought her a small orchard spray and with this she shot a warm mist over the old paper, let it sink in, and then she and the girl took putty knives and worked the paper off. It went fairly fast and was less expensive than hiring a steamer and then finding somebody to run it. One of the most depressing things which was borne in on me, in the progress of my awakening to the real difficulties of regeneration, was my discovery that those following trades lacked professional integrity. It was not merely that any given craftsman—the word of course has lost all meaning—was unethical. Skill was gone, pride in the work; he was not even interested much in his pay, for the war and the government had diverted the workmen from a belief in that basic fear of want which stiffens the social morality in good times and makes all men of family remember the diversity of evil. This condition was not entirely the fault of those in public places; they were merely the representatives of this democracy of absolute corruption, for the evil had long been working in the yeast. Everywhere one felt a spiritual emasculation, for a man's final belief in himself comes from his attitude toward and his performance of his job. The soldier must be given ice cream to fight, all the rest of us must be bribed to live, for after all in spite of the conspiracy of silence and ignorance we, the impious, do know fear, the fear of those who sin against the Holy Ghost, the pretense that matter is all and that he who looks on the act of creation is himself creator.

As I came downstairs, I found Ellen in the great hall. She was alone, sitting on the floor, in the midst of the debris of strips of wallpaper and the tools she was using—putty knives, stepladders, pans of water and patching plaster. Doors back and front were open and a warm breeze had already dried the top layer of the dirty brown paper. She seemed small and fragile and not the occasion for the litter but some rare object, so still was she, which should have been moved before the work began but had been overlooked by careless eyes. Her own eyes looked toward the door but they had the bright gaze of preoccupation. She did not hear me as I came up.

I said softly, "A penny for your thoughts."

"Oh," she said. "It is you."

"You seem overwhelmed by your work."

"No, I was thinking about a time long ago, when I was sixteen."

"That's not so long, darling."

"It's centuries ago. My grandmother gave me a hat, I remember. It was my birthday. I thought it the most beautiful hat in the world. It had daisies underneath the brim and a soft blue ribbon which tied in a bow. How I walked and turned before the mirror! The world was very beautiful that day." And then she said sadly, "I never see daisies now that are half so pretty."

After a second I said, "Where is Maybelle? I thought she was helping."

"I had some things to wash. I'd rather do this than wash."

"You should have called me."

She rose with a little sigh. "It's rather a relief to

get rid of you for a while." She said this pleasantly enough, but what is said in jest is often meant for earnest. "You've been sticking like a leech, you know. And I can't get any work out of you."

"I thought you liked me around."

"I do, but much better as a hand than watcher." She grew serious. "I don't know whatever possessed you to think you would like to do over this old place. You avoid the simplest job. It's lots of fun doing things together. Not much doing it alone." She smiled wryly. "I don't ask you any more. You groan so it takes all the pleasure away."

"You know that's not so," I said. "I want things to improve."

"You did once." She was facing me gravely, almost in accusation. "This is our home. We live here. We are putting our things here. Your things in a sense are you." And then she came out with it: "What is it that makes you loathe everything you do?"

This struck me like a bolt out of the blue. I felt that swollen clarity all blows give, and the incapacity to act. Mechanically I picked up the patching plaster and a putty knife and turned to the bare wall. It was my way of retreat.

"Now I've hurt its feelings," she said.

"I'm completely crushed," I replied.

This feeble effort at facetiousness failed, but it gave me time. And I needed time in which to recover from the surprise of this attack. It was so unlike Ellen. It was alien, hostile, the author of this exposure. But it

117

was no stranger. I knew him well but not so well as he knew me, or I should have stopped this great forward stride of his. If I lacked proof before of communication between them, I had it now. Ellen was too close to me to discover so revolutionary a change in feeling, a change which I myself, until the shock brought me the truth, was unaware of. It was true. I was beginning to loathe everything about *The Grove,* for the place had become the symbol of the waste of our lives, the subversion of my one idea.

As the putty knife flew down the cracks in the plaster, I could feel the look of defeat withdraw behind my eyes. The motion of my hands relieved me. My balance was restored, but I had to get out of the house. I had to move about. I turned and said, "Let's go into the garden and see what progress Johnny has made."

"But there's still so much to do here."

"We can't do it all in a day," I countered. "We are jugglers, you know. We have many balls in the air. To drop one is to lose the game." Strange words, and irrelevant, I thought, as I heard myself easily start a conversation so unrelated to my thoughts.

She took it up.

"It *is* rather like a circus, isn't it?"

"So it is. I will change the metaphor. I'm the tight-rope walker."

"And I, the lady bareback rider?"

"No, darling, you are still the juggler."

"But are there lady jugglers?"

"Well, yes, and no. The juggler might—I say might—slip into a lady's skin."

"What fun for the lady!"

"And for the juggler."

"Oh," she said in mock withdrawal, "I shouldn't think it would be fun for him at all."

"No fun for the juggler?" I asked with lifted brow.

"No fun for the juggler. He has to keep the balls in the air."

She laughed gaily and I joined in, rather wryly, and then I said, "One reflects the company one keeps."

"You see then," she replied, "what an effect you are having on me these days."

"I, Mrs. Brent?"

She gave me a direct stare and, to be sure I did not miss her meaning, added, "Who else, Mr. Brent?"

CHAPTER NINETEEN

HERE is no ruin so definitive as one that has been cleared of debris. A dead city covered by silt or jungle takes on the anonymity of nature. Dig it out and you apprehend more than you would looking at a city crowded with the commerce of men. What you actually encounter is the ruin of life. All that man was and tried to be lies exposed in the bareness of the broken structure. The tremendous effort to exist and to persist finds there its ironic commentary. One dares not look too long.

As I came up to the garden, now cleaned of rubbish and undergrowth, an impression of personal and private ruin swept over me. The exposure was sudden and complete: the brick in the walks were uneven where roots had traveled; the borders of the flower beds showed a few scraggly box; here and there a rosebush grew out of shape. At the center the rotten floor of the springhouse looked crumbly and gray from the drying sun let in after so many years. All over, the garden was studded with the fresh-cut stems of bushes, like stobs driven in upside down. But the design, as a whole and in detail, was sharp and as importunate as a

120

whispered message. And yet nothing had been restored. I could tell that Johnny had done, for him, a
good job and one, as he probably thought, suitable for
the occasion. He could not reach the bulging roots beneath the brick walks, and it was plain that what nature
had marred would remain forever misshapen. It occurred to me that he had cleaned it as he would have
cleaned a family burying ground for a reunion of the
descendants, giving the place a general tidying up but
leaving the sunken graves and broken headstones
strictly alone.

"Why do you stop at the gate?" Ellen asked, inter-
rupting my brown study. "It was you who would see
it this time of day."

"Yes, I know," I said. "It was I."

"Well, then, won't you ask me to come into the garden?"

"Will you come with me into the garden, Miss Ellen,
where it is always midsummer?"

"How poetic, Mr. Brent!"

"Not at all, Miss Ellen."

"But indeed, Mr. Brent."

"Midsummer," I mused. "Nature's deceiving pause.
Come walk with me there."

"Haven't you mixed your seasons? Summer is
past."

"In a flower garden there is only one season, Miss
Ellen. The time of blooming."

"But flowers fade—" and she raised her arms melo-
dramatically—"even here."

"Ah, yes. But one does not notice. That is the art of the garden, to have it always in bloom."

"A very pretty illusion."

"So that the progress of the seasons goes unnoted."

"I don't follow," she said, taking my arm.

"Consider the garden well, my dear. It has many uses, but first and always one thinks of love."

"Naturally."

"Don't you mean romantically?"

"Exactly. You are very quick today."

"And so . . ."

"Romantic love denies the seasonal return. It is a pretense, a love for love's sake, an aesthetic pretense, if you will. And for setting, the garden forever in bloom, forever withholding its seed."

"What a lovely illusion and how utterly barren! You were not so learned when you courted me." And then abruptly changing her tone, "How wonderful it would be if the garden were now in bloom, if it could have always remained what it was, and not its poor distraught self!"

"You see why I wanted to keep this for last."

"Oh, but I couldn't wait," she said in a strange tight voice. And then more calmly, "Thank you for having Johnny begin it."

"Well, there he is. Thank him yourself."

We went around to the far side of the springhouse where Johnny was. Ellen said, "You've done a wonderful job, Johnny."

He acknowledged this praise. "Hit taken right smart sprouten, Miss Ellen. We ain't made the show here we aimed to. Look lak we couldn't grub clost to the ground thout taring somethen up." He looked about him with measuring eye. "You can't rightly say that this war a hot-weather job noways. I reckon me and the boys done moved forty families' trash."

"It's a lovely spot," she said. "I shall spend a lot of time here."

"Hit war oncet a place for a body to take his ease in," he said, wiping his forehead and putting his hat back on. "But hit'll might nigh take one hand's time to keep the trash down now."

"Oh dear, do you think so?"

He reflected: "Hit'll last out this year, we being in the dog days."

"I think it's the loveliest plan for a garden."

Johnny responded as if the compliment were paid him personally.

"Major Brent war a man for sich as this. He a man to step around in sweet-smellen places. No matter how hard he drove heself, when he come to the house first thing right off he washed. He washed his har in scented ile and chewed spices."

"What a man!" Ellen said. I glanced her way. It was plain she delighted in hearing his name.

"Yes'm, in many ways. Excusen me, he was a great hand with the ladies. He used to promenade 'm here a sight."

Ellen did not reply to this. I said, "So he was a ladies' man?"

"In his sappy days, you might say he was a sporten man." Johnny indicated the walkways with a gesture. "He laid hit out like a race track. And promenaded 'm round and round. When he taken the notion, he'd stop and pick a bokay of sweet bubbies."

"I should think," Ellen said rather testily, "the ladies would have got dizzy, going around in circles."

"I've heared it made some of um faintified," Johnny reported gravely.

There was nothing forward in his manner or expression as he said this, but Ellen did not like it. She took a step to end the conversation. Johnny reached out his hand. "Take care, Miss Ellen."

"What?" she said sharply.

"Hit's bad luck to step over a grave."

"Grave?" she asked and looked wonderingly at her feet.

"Grave?" I repeated.

"Yessir." Johnny pointed to the flat stone top of an outdoor tomb. "He didn't lay out no burying ground at *The Grove*," he continued simply. "He knowed he wouldn't need nairn for heseff. He just laid um all away in the garden here."

"All?" we asked in surprise.

"He wives," Johnny replied with just the proper degree of pride and respect. "Yes'm, he laid 'm out lak spokes in a wheel, all around the springhouse. All six of um."

"What a Bluebeard!" Ellen said.

Johnny looked at Ellen for a moment. "Maybe a tech of blue. He beard war black as sin."

Ellen was down on her knees reading the inscription on the tomb.

"Six, Johnny?" I asked. "I'd forgotten there were so many."

"Yessir. I come acrost um under the bresh here." He gazed into the air. "I calls 'm his wives."

"You what?"

Silently Ellen passed from grave to grave, reading the inscriptions. Johnny followed her with his eyes for some moments, then said, "Miss Jane war the first un. Her chillurn all growed and scattered. He got Miss Sally in Montgomery County. She died. Miss Lizzie come from somewheres off. When she died, look lak he lost heart in visiting ladies in a proper kind of way. The rest of um jest kept house for him." He threw this off in a matter-of-fact way, seemed to meditate, and then said, "Look lak, whether from fenced ground or off the commons, hit didn't agree with um none too well here."

By now Ellen had completed the circle. She was standing on the other side of the springhouse, rather straight, her face pale, her head up like a startled animal. But it was the eyes which alarmed me. For the first time I saw fright in them, but there was something besides fright. She was like one who, eating of a strange and rich dish, looks up suddenly with the knowledge that it is poisoned. "The poor dears," she whispered. "All but one died in childbed." And then without looking at either me or Johnny, she walked rapidly out of the garden.

Johnny and I remained a long time quiet. "No, sir," I heard him say at last, "hit jest didn't noways agree with um at *The Grove*. Some folks 'lowed they was too frail."

"What do you allow?" I asked.

"Nothen," Johnny replied.

Never did I hear so much put into one short word.

CHAPTER TWENTY.

I KNEW the moment Ellen left the garden that we all faced a fresh crisis. I even felt that I had the obvious chance to draw her back from the abyss where she tottered. But I could make the wrong move and send her plunging down beyond all reach, forever beyond hope of redemption. Still there was hope—I held to this—hope in the inkling she had gained of the sinister nature of the past. She had been dazzled by a mirage cast up for her in the arid reaches of the mind where she had lost the way. But there in the garden her eyes had been opened. She more than suspected the horrors she was drifting toward. She more than believed in their reality. I had seen it in her face withdrawing from the circle of the flat-topped graves. I heard the words "died in childbed." Those women had died; it suited the experience of that time to say of child. But Ellen asked, Six dead women—why?

The next move was mine, to seize upon this doubt, to show her the ghastly meaning of this warning from the grave. Was it an entirely unconscious slip that she had referred to Major Brent as a Bluebeard? I thought not. I must make the most of this before the colored mist of her bemusement again settled and she followed the way of its frightful promise. But how? I stayed awake into the small hours thinking of all possible ways to approach her. So far there had been only allusions to her ghostly intercourse. Her replies had been masterly in evasion. Upon them I hung alternately between hope and despair. But throughout this entanglement of half-formed decisions and uncertainties I held fast to one clear fact: so long as she was willing to play such a game she was unsure of herself. She had not quite tired of the world and me. This was one way of looking at it. There was another, much darker and altogether disheartening. Suppose she was already his creature and taunted me out of the slavery of her surrender? Perhaps it was weakness to deny this possibility, but deny it I did. What I had learned in the garden gave me fresh courage. But I must work fast. The time had come to take the risk of judgment, to call a spade a spade—and a ghost a ghost.

I slipped into my dressing gown, my dragon gown of eastern silk, and made my way to the little sitting room next to our sleeping quarters. Her door was shut. All was quiet beyond. Should I arouse her to disburden my mind? Would this frighten her and thwart my desire? I could not stand to see in my anxious state that mask she now wore so often. To succeed I must see her. As I hung there in indecision, it was solved for me on the instant. I knew as clearly as if I had heard words spoken, that something awaited me outside.

I fairly floated into the corridor in the wonder of this knowledge. Even now, after all that has happened, and when the end is known, the miraculous quality of my sensation, the feeling of security and power it gave me, returns to haunt me. In that moment I experienced the irreducible essence of self, the mystery understood by all at death, that ecstasy of the spirit which a few religious glimpse in their contempt for matter but which I discovered as the absolute purity of selfhood. The gross weight of my body melted as jelly does in water, bone, muscle, and flesh no longer governed by but become that which is indestructible. You may call it illusion, but I say that for that particular pause in time I was the subject of a miracle. I stood for a moment at my threshold, but who can name the true name of the threshold I had reached? The night was dark and cloudy and a smell of distant rain freshened the air. The murky light of the moon streaked the edge of a cloud. Then like a young hound I struck the scent.

I can think of no better term. Some presence, hovering near, had passed. The trail it left was still sweet. That is the hunter's phrase and I was become a hunter. How shall I describe it? For one thing, it showed a definite direction but moved on a wavering line, such as air waves do. If anyone had seen me, he would have thought I was drunk and staggering to my room. There was of course no physical trail. There was nothing but the smell of moist air, and yet my nostrils flared, although I scarcely breathed, as they would have done at a scent blown past in a high gale. Curiously enough, what I remember best about it is the feeling of heaviness, almost of matter. I followed as one is drawn along the heavy footing of a dream. It swirled about my ankles in the slow heavy way of mist clinging to low places. Once I looked down, but saw nothing. I felt I could touch but could not touch it; could see but did not see it; could smell but did not smell it. I followed.

I neither rushed nor delayed. I walked with the sure, absolute balance of a somnambulant, and I walked unafraid. The darkness did not confuse. Nothing confused, nothing obstructed me. My earth-bound senses had all perished in the miraculous transformation they had undergone. I had now one sense, the sense of myself.

And all the while the night held dark, but my vision ate into it like acid. Along the back corridor I followed until I came to the small enclosed passage connecting the south end of the apartment to the upstairs hall. It was close, narrow, and rather poorly lighted even by day. At night one hurried through it with a childish feeling of unknown terror. And always at this hour the outside door was locked; yet I knew it would open to my hand. The door jumped at me; the scent, a thousandfold stronger, enveloped me.

I had no thought now but of Ellen's peril. I rushed to her door, but once there I noticed that the effluvium lay more heavily toward the opening into the hall. Why should it sweep to the very threshold of her room and then veer off? There was one plausible answer. She was even now being sucked along in its tow.

I hurried into the hall, but what I entered was a place deeper and broader than any hallway. Before me was the balcony. Its door was flung back and there I saw, with arms hanging limply, steps advancing in hypnotic tread toward the rotten balcony rail, not Ellen, but poor bemused Moss.

CHAPTER TWENTY-ONE

*I*WAS too far away. I could only watch the mechanical impulsion of his advance, the slight twist of the head as if he were straining toward something in the distance. I saw him fumble at the rotten banister, then put his hand lightly on the railing. Still like one who sees nothing close by, he raised his leg in even motion. This broke my spell. I called his name sharply. He hesitated, dipped his head as if to miss an obstacle; then proceeded to carry on the interrupted action. . . . I heard the wood give a long straining creak. It was not until this moment of peril that my voice got through to him. He shuddered, took a step back from the open space and slowly turned, as if still reluctant to give over whatever image it was that had drawn him so close to disaster.

I was carried forward on the upsurge of my relief. Relief . . . the sweetness of danger passed. Afterward there comes a lift to the simplest thing. The hall seemed its familiar self, its walls safe and comforting. I even forgot the threat to the peace of the house. The gruff thunder rumbling in the distance gave off a friendly sound. But I needed some physical reassurance. The residue of nerves had left in my body a dull swollen ache. Desperately I felt the need to hug Moss. I took a step toward him . . . and then the moon plunged into the clear. Under the slow spread of its light, the tops of trees grew sharply dark, the lawn appeared vaguely familiar, and there upon it an amorphous blotch of shadow, as though secretly slipping out of the picture, took on line and form, the head first, then the long body, and at last the insolent set of the legs I knew so well. There in all his evil stood Major Brent, his head thrown back into the light. The face, fixed on the balcony, still and glistening, showed in its hideous nakedness his purpose, a purpose the intent of which was already changing into triumph, as if he were sure of his victim. My eyes slowly dimmed and then went out. When I looked again, he had vanished. The moon had gone under a cloud, and the world was everywhere dark.

I felt myself step back against the wall for support. The five senses, somewhat flagging, had resumed their natural functions. "Well," I said wearily, "how did it happen? If I had been twenty seconds later, you would be lying on the bricks below." And then out of my exasperation, "How did he manage it?"

"How did who manage what?" I heard softly, almost mockingly.

I was in no mood for this. "For God's sake, boy, this is no time for evasions. How did he beguile you? What did he say? What do? You must try to remember."

"Beguile me?" Moss was all youth and confidence,

with some bravado, as he returned me this question.

"Yes, Major Brent beguiled you," I said flatly.

"Major Brent?" he repeated as though the name came as an impossible surprise. "I've not seen your Major Brent." And then as if there were some need to emphasize his statement, "I have never seen your Major Brent."

I truly at this stage, pressed as I was with the increased pace of the drama we were enacting, felt that I had more than I could bear. It was possible that Moss's memory had been wiped clean . . . unless—I must always face this uncertainty—unless the enemy's insidious promises had some way made the victim accessory to the crime.

"Perhaps you were dreaming and walked in your sleep," I said to help him along.

"No," he replied blandly, "I am here because I want to be here."

His tone irritated me beyond bearing. I did not stop to reflect that this tone had been set by some prior command left in the consciousness for just this effect. I could only blurt out, and the harshness of my voice rebounded like an echo, "Well, but for me, you would be lost in it."

"In your mind, Uncle, I am already lost," he replied.

"I have not said it."

I could think of no reply. I had again been taken by surprise.

"No, but you think it."

"Of course I don't," I answered rather lamely, if

134

truthfully, for what I did think came close to the same thing. But how could he know this unless he had been taught to read my mind just as Ellen had been taught, when she accused me of hating everything I did at *The Grove*.

There was nothing for me to do but to come right out with it. "No, Moss," I said. "But you have been keeping something back. This is the hour for truth. Why do you hide here?"

"What makes you think I am hiding?"

It was all so frankly outspoken, not only what he said but his manner of speech, that I felt as if I were deliberately creating a mysterious situation out of a natural circumstance. I didn't carry much conviction, saying, "Well, by the way you arrived here, for one thing."

"Didn't you expect me?"

"I did."

"Well, then."

How in the wrong I felt as I pushed it further, "I mean the way you appeared. You will admit it was unusual."

"But didn't you want me?"

"Of course." But I didn't let this clever flattery divert me. "You came here, a remote place. You didn't go to your father's house, where you would be known."

"I can't go home. I can come only to you," he said.

"But why?"

"You know why," he said.

I didn't know how to push this further. In his clever

way he knew it, and he knew that I knew it. I changed my approach. "And the way you have kept hidden, coming out only at night. Sleeping by day."

"But that was your idea, Uncle."

This was a half-truth but it silenced me. My delicacy in the matter, from the sympathy between us which had led me to understand his predicament and not press him with it, now rendered me helpless. As I said no more, he drove me farther into my corner. "It was you, you know, who chose the daytime watch."

This wound me up and tied me off. What proof is there to a silent agreement, if one party refuses to honor it? What face I would have lost if I had given away to temper, before so much youth and candor and the innocent-seeming pleasure he took in catching me in his net. I could imagine the look of hurt and surprise in the soft dark eyes, the injured query and afterward the awkward drop of the head, for he liked to please and never had he been one to bear correction. This was the lesson I had learned and his father had not.

No, I had to accept the shift in our relations and act, when the need arose, within the new limits imposed. As we parted, I parted with the deeper knowledge of the enemy's skill and the fresh ground I had lost.

CHAPTER TWENTY-TWO

*T*HERE are times when the best of us falter, when we feel sorry for ourselves. I had reached that hazardous state: I felt very sorry for myself. If I had been a man of deliberate evil, there would be some justice to the ordeal I was being put through. But what was I? Can any man answer this question? I tried to, in the chill of those before-dawn hours after I had left Moss. I left him with a good conscience. I was sure Major Brent would return no more that night, but indeed I was so low in mind that if he had, I would have said, Enter your domain and do your will. At least I think I would.

Where I wandered I do not know. My steps moved in reflex action to the real journey which went on in my head. And that took me down past the will, past the imagination, to the obscure area which the soul inhabits. Here there are limpid patches where lights play, but all else is opaque and of an endless depth no resources can plumb. But I probed as well as I could. Like two boys shouting threats across the circle of dust their fears are treading, I went round myself, and only when shame turned fear into pain did I suffer knowledge. Knowledge, the memory of where we go

137

wrong but never quite why. There are two questions
that may be put—What and How. The scientist asks
What, the artist How, but in any case both burn in the
same fire. The residue of one is ashes for the winds,
the leavings of the other a thing of hard irreducible
form, telling all and nothing, and its polish is the shine
of agony. My agony was in the making, but who can
leap clear of the fire, that leap which hurries time and
rushes the end?

I had come to live at *The Grove,* for in my blood was
the insistent need to abide. The wanderer wears smooth
as a penny and tells fortunes, but never his own. The
gypsy in the coonskin cap, making always his circle—
this I fled and sought the place where the seasons
make their orderly return, to the dwelling for the
woman, to the earth for the seed, and I to my care. I
came to a place with a western view. I was not the
prodigal returning to the fatted calf, and yet there was
one who saw me from afar, but he did not rush forth
and fall on my neck. He waited and when I came I
found a thing out of time haunting the mouldering
bones. I found that the body has its seasons, too, and
that they are brief and, diminutive of the great seasons,
make one cycle.

And so it is that the great fear is not death but oblivion. And oblivion settles on an impotent man. It was
this, I decided, which had kept Major Brent near the
scene of his crime, for impotence has a larger meaning
than the body's lack. In vanity and by will he had cut
off his line; or so he had intended, but there he fell into

radical error. Call it metaphysical if you will, but the progeny *The Grove* might rightfully claim as its due had gone to the grave with Major Brent. But it would not lie. A thing must live before it dies. And this progeny, forbidden life, drew back the shade of Major Brent and fastened him to the air of the place. Its mortal weight forbade him the felicitous reaches of infinity. To be neither of the world nor altogether out of it—that was his punishment. I had got this much, wandering through the tortured night, and I knew I had got it right. But it was not with this I had to do.

I will state it plainly. Every crime demands expiation, every expiation a victim. That he might go free, dispossess himself of the blur of mortality, Major Brent had chosen what I loved for victim. The nature of the sacrifice was not clear to me at this time, but my fears grew out of its very vagueness, for I knew it was not vague to him. I had seen enough this night to know that his ghostly purpose had advanced almost to the moment of resolution. I must steady myself for the last onset he, even now, had withdrawn to loose. I probed no more. As I entered Ellen's room, our room, I had decided: we would flee *The Grove* before it was too late.

The night lamp by her bed was lighted.

"You are awake," I said.

The shadows from the lamp showed me only half her face, and the thin gown, falling over her frail shoulders and exposing the round breast, seemed already shadowy light withdrawing into deeper shade. "You are awake,"

I said again and crossed the room to turn up the lamp.

"What time is it?" she asked.

"Late or early. The roosters are crowing."

"They often crow at midnight. I think the deep stillness of sleep startles them, and they cry out that it is sleep, that it may be broken."

"It is after midnight," I said.

"Is it?" she said dreamily, looking all the while at my face, but I felt that her sight focused on some reverie of phantoms I was sure she now met with urgent, feverish need. Then suddenly her eyes became clearer and she said, "What are you doing up at this hour?"

"I might ask, Why are you awake?"

"I couldn't sleep. I've been thinking."

"About what?"

"About us and what we do here."

"For instance?"

"Well, for one thing, about you wandering at night, not coming to bed."

"Did I wake you?"

"Something did."

I sat on the bed and took her hand. I asked very slowly, "Do you know what it was?"

"Why, no," she said and yet this answer seemed to imply that I could tell her if I would.

I leaned slightly forward, as her attention was about to waver. "Do you know where it was?"

"Why, no. Why do you look so strange?"

I pinned her down. "Are you sure?"

"Well, no . . . yes." I felt her hand withdrawing from mine, but I held it fast. "I thought there was something out there. I couldn't be sure."

"Where?" I was calm, but oh, how insistent! "In the hall, perhaps?"

"Perhaps. You were in the hall, weren't you? Let go my hand. You are hurting me." She pulled away and said, "Have you seen anything?"

Go carefully, carefully, I warned myself. You cannot say you have seen a ghost and let her laugh the truth off, even though the laugh cry out in harsh falsity. I said, "The night is full of things, if you can see in the dark."

"Can you see in the dark, dear? I can't. I light a lamp."

We were now back at our old evasions, which skimmed the surface of the thing we feared to name, but which by the very lightness of innuendo admitted its presence.

"Are you afraid of what you will see in the dark?" I asked.

"But I've just told you. I make a light. A light is a comfort to a lonely woman. Yet it makes her more lonely."

"Are you so much alone?" I said directly, dropping the banter.

"I have been. You see, you either work or wander around the place like a man with a bad conscience. You should have a bad conscience neglecting me as you do."

"But does it matter so much to you?" I asked leaning closer.

I had driven her into a corner. She looked away as if to escape and I pitied her with all my heart. If I could only have helped! But it was not for me to help. After a moment she collected herself. Her breath made a fast little gallop.

"Yes, it has mattered," she said. "But it may not any more."

Her voice and eyes were deliberately teasing; and then she came out with it so easily and with such self-confidence I almost felt in her the demand for my sympathy and approval. "There may be someone, you know, to take your place."

You may expect the worst and think you are prepared, but you are never prepared. The prisoner at the dock is never prepared, even though he reads his doom in the judge's face. The few simple words seem too slight for the finality of their intelligence. You cannot move. You sit motionless, with the sense of the stricken years between you like a glass and in the hall below the clock strikes the hour. You sit as though you would sit out time until the last stroke of the gong dies away and you rise and passionately take her in your arms and there is a gasp of pain in her breath and you say, "I will take you away from this haunted house."

She does not speak, though your desperate embrace bruises and you sense fear in her rapid breath, fear of what she does not understand in you, fear that she will be torn from the phantom who grows in her desire like a cancer. Then at last the strength goes from your grasp and you release her and she draws back against the headboard, with the fright now seen in her eyes and behind the wide iris resistance growing. You hear your dull words, dulled from the expense of passion, "How was I to know?"

After a while, when she sees your strength abate, she stirs slightly, but speaks clearly enough, "Where do you think you can take me?"

"Anywhere away from this."

"Do you think it will help to go away? There was a time for that, but that time is past."

"Time passes," I said vehemently, "but you make time too. I brought you here, but how was I to know what I would find?" And then I blurted out, for my words catching fire from themselves leaped trembling and out of control, "I'm afraid I'll lose you."

"That," she said quietly, "is a risk you must take."

I had expected denials, derision, some guilty mask behind which she might retreat, I don't know what I expected, anything but the surprise I got, the one thing that would silence me, this challenge to my manhood. And it was not only her words, but the manner she assumed, a quiet resignation, such open courageous frankness, such gleaming sorrow, how shall I describe the strength and weakness she seemed, except to say that she presented the devoted look of the victim, that fusion of innocence and desire which makes ecstatic the eye of the sinner as he ravishes and cleans himself upon what his glance devours.

But I was not that sinner. I was the one from whose arms she had been snatched by lot, and as I stood there, for a moment helpless, all my old longing for her love, the keener for the sense of the loss I would suffer, took hold of me. "No love shall supplant our love," I whispered, advancing.

"No, no," she said, drawing back. "Don't ruin everything."

But I did not hear. My hand pressed on the hot circle the lamp chimney made. The light flickered and then went out. For an instant the tongue of flame leaped at my flesh. My mouth swam in hot jets of pain and the silence swelled into one great swoon. She for a little resisted my arms, but at last I plunged into darkness.

CHAPTER TWENTY-THREE

*M*ORNING seemed eternities away. As did the day of our marriage when I waited for her at the chancel and she came forward as a beautiful woman toward a looking glass. There is no act of darkness so desperate that daylight may not compromise it. But how the dawn delayed! I could almost believe it conspired with the night, so dismally did it creep out of the east, behind a dew that was more fog than dew.

What folly made me think that violence could draw love back but the folly of desperation? Whoever finds again what he has lost? What wanderer returning home finds other than exile in the familiar landmark? Yet the loser seeks, the wanderer returns, and I must do what I had to do. I could smell the greasy stain of the lamp chimney as I sat on the bed's edge, waiting for enough resolution to get up and salvage what I could from the night's despair. I saw my scattered clothes on the floor and felt afresh that vast distance the quietness made between us, after the dry sobs, and the dead voice, "How could you do this?" And then in bitter wonderment, "How could you?" How could she not understand? I learned easily enough how one may maim what one loves. But that was the night. The light of day now seeped into the room. I reached for my clothes. They pricked like cold needles.

Outside the damp air brought me up to action. This day we would flee the place. First I would deal with Moss. He would get around me with no more equivocation. He must confront his secret and resolve it. I crossed to the old office where he stayed and entered without knocking. The smudge at the dirty window gave enough light to show me his bed had not been slept in. I drew closer to make sure. There was not a wrinkle on the counterpane. It had the cold, starched look of a bed made up for the casual guest. And then on the instant I discovered how far behind events were leaving me. The moldy, shut-up smell of disuse told me that Moss had never used his room.

There was not a moment to lose. I hurried toward Johnny's house and met him with a lantern on his way to the barn. The fog was so heavy he didn't see me until I was almost upon him, but he gave no sign of surprise. He stopped, hunched up with the chill, and waited. "Take me right now," I said, "to the spot where Major Brent looked over the fields for the last time."

He gave the lantern to one of the daughters. She moved off like a shadow and the fog enveloped her. One by one his boys passed, their bulks thinning until they, too, disappeared. I said, "We must hurry. We may even now be too late."

Johnny kept my pace, without seeming to increase the slow steady swing of the countryman. "I've just come from my nephew's room. He did not sleep there last night."

"Young folks runs at night," he said.

"I saw him last night. I saw whom he was with."

We went along and I said no more to let this sink in. There was no sound but the rub of my corduroys. "He was with our friend," I said significantly. I waited a few steps more, then: "I arrived in time to save him."

"What he want wid him?" he blurted out.

I half turned, but Johnny kept his glance before him, as if he were intent on not losing the way. "I thought *you* might tell *me*," I said. By slowing my words I gave them the emphasis of an accusation. "You tend his room. You must know he hasn't used it."

Then Johnny did a surprising thing. He delayed his pace as if from indecision; then stopped and for an instant looked directly into my eyes. "Boss, you knows who him's after."

He turned away and resumed walking. His glance did not rest long enough on mine for me to make an issue of it, but I felt such a chill of revelation on the profundities of my situation that, of necessity, I sought for some superficial evasion. I dared not ask who. For days I was to be haunted by the depths within depths of his dark pupils swimming in those eyeballs the color of eggshell. They saw. What did they foresee?

The mist was lifting. It gave me my excuse. We came to a field where the fences had rotted down and upon the edges of gulleys the washed field showed thin and red. A fury seized me at this evidence of Major Brent's will. I turned upon Johnny. "You haven't cleaned out these fence rows."

"Naw sir. Look like a body never do ketch up."

"They've grown at least forty feet into this field."

"They's still plenty ground."

What good now to tell him I had come to save and restore, now that I had thrown in the sponge and was leaving? But the evidence of my defeat was so flagrant I could not help saying, "This is what Major Brent wanted. To turn this place into a wilderness."

"He done it now," he replied in what I thought was a completely irrelevant tone.

"I came here," I said bitterly, "to make it so you and everybody at *The Grove* could have a more abundant life."

"'Bundance?" I could almost hear his mind turning the word over. "You means meat aplenty in the smoke-house?"

"In a way, yes."

"I ain't never knowed the time." We went along for a while, I still mad and he . . . he said presently, his voice keeping time to his stride, "But looks lak time I burns my plant beds and sows 'm I ain't turned round good befo'e they needs setten. I works hit, suckers it, worms it, tops hit, cuts hit and hangs it in the barn. I ain't got my breaf good befo'e got to haul barn wood and fire hit. When the order's right got to git it down. Strip hit. Bulk hit. Then time comes to sell and you feels you done yo'ese'f a favor. You stands round waiten and the buyers and the pinhookers comes in jesten, and they strolls along, picks up a hand and flings hit down, and the man callen Hi, yi, yi . . . Sold. And nar, befo'e you kin spit, you been hiyied out'n a year's work." He paused. "No, sir. A body just ain't got no time for 'bundance."

No time for abundance. What has man time for? I should have asked, but what was the good now of struggling with his inertia? I did not even pause for bitterness. We walked on and under the sun the mist burned away and I saw we had reached a large woods. I said, "Which way?"

Johnny nodded before him. "That hit."

I did not understand. "That's what?"

"Whar you wanted me to bring you."

"That's no field," I cried in sudden panic.

"No, sir. Not no more hit ain't."

Even now I was slow to accept what I saw, so blinded was I by that image of golden fields abandoned to rot. There is the act, and there is the image of the act. But the slow turn of the seasons fills out the truth. I gazed at the buckbushes, the tangle of brush and briers and overhead the leaves of autumn shifting their masses of color, now showing, now hiding, the anonymous depths of the wilderness. "Let's hurry," I said.

Johnny drew back his foot. "This here is fur as I goes."

"What do you mean?"

"I ain't *never* been in them woods."

149

"But if I go . . ."

"That ain't me."

I said slowly, "Do you mean you are **abandoning** me, here and now?"

He looked up and down; said, "Hit make a body squinty-eyed to look at what you sees."

"Very well," I replied. "I'll go alone."

To this he gave no reply, nor did I look at him again. I started in, fearing but sure of what I would find there, not knowing whether I should be too late. The briers struck and bound me in their sharp festoons.

Johnny called out, "The cattle uses sometimes below."

"Why didn't you tell me?" I called back in exasperation.

I found the break the cattle had made and followed the faint and winding path. Along this I hurried, dodging the slapping limbs until I found myself well in among the trees. Here I left the path, for it followed a simple instinctive route and, being cattle-made, would skirt the center where I was going. I took direction as well as my haste would allow and pushed on. It was not a large wood, that is not large enough to get lost in, but it was dense and had reached the season which is life-in-death. The black gums, the first to turn, appeared through the green depths, great bloody flowers already drying, and on the fresher leaves a faint brush of yellow cast everywhere its blight. This confused my eyes, but I plunged along, choosing the easiest ground until at last I found I had lost the way.

If I had stopped calmly to take my bearings, it would have been a matter of minutes before I should have come close to the center. But the urgent need, the waste of time, and my bewilderment drove me on. Beneath my trousers I could feel the smart of brier and thorn; my shoes grew slick; I slipped and fell.

Weary and smarting, I paused half-blind with sweat and despair. I saw how deep a way in I had gone, for all about me the light grew even. There came an instant when I almost heard the woods catch its breath. It grew as still as quail in a brush pile. To the depths of this quiet my solitude abandoned me. I had suffered at *The Grove,* I would suffer yet again, but there was nothing to equal the terror of this solitude. Then out of it I heard a steady rhythm of breathing. I have no way of knowing when it began. I can only know that at some certain moment it must have begun. It was a sound such as one might hear in a dream, the surprise of its imminence when you first grow aware of it. But here in the woods I at once thought of some cornered beast. Yet a beast would have made no sound. It seemed to come from a clump of bushes close at hand. But it was not there. I heard it behind me. I turned, and it turned also. No matter where I looked, it was always somewhere else, yet always near. I began to run, now completely at hazard. What stopped me was the insolent, almost human complaint of crows startled on their perches. I looked up in time to see one swift black streak before it vanished, cawing, among the leaves. I looked down and saw my nephew Moss.

151

He was in a part of the woods more open than the rest, and his back was to me. I had only a moment, but I needed only a moment to feel the hard tight lump of pain in the throat and that terrible drop into emptiness which accompanied it. I had only to see the set of his back, his absorbing gaze, the force of which came to me as clearly as if I had seen it, to know that I had lost him. There was not much to go by, but the heart needs very little. He was erect through all the lean vigor of his person, but the tension in his shoulders told me volumes. They showed an extravagant long-ing for abandonment. All of this—what I felt and saw—fused in a flash of intuition, for I had no more than seen him before he began to move away. I cried out in my misery, "Stop! Wait!" but he was deaf to my appeal. I ran forward to seize him, to save him in spite of himself, but I was thrown back—the place was truly enchanted—by a barrier of thorn trees that struck deep into my flesh. When I had got around these, he was gone. I followed, running and stopping, in the direction I supposed he had taken. I called his name; but the deep hush, more hostile for my noisy progress through it, gave back no reply. He had liter-ally vanished before my eyes. Or so I thought until, a few paces farther on, I parted the bushes and came out on the rim of a sinkhole.

It was a large sinkhole, great enough to have pulled small trees down its rotten sides. For a moment I hesitated; then my eyes followed down the slope to the black gaping opening at the bottom. I shuddered and because action was the only thing that would save me, I made my way down the steep slick sides. For the last five yards there was neither purchase nor bush to hold to. There I stopped. There I faced the door to mystery. Fascinated and repelled, I looked into the black emptiness below me. One glance was enough: the hole was easily big enough for a man to fall through. In the silence which my long gaze made I heard the ominous sound of water running underground.

How long I remained staring I do not know, long enough to feel the dangerous pull of that subterranean sound, promising release, escape from the unbearable, the lull of utter rest and oblivion. What saved me, reminding me that I had another to protect, came from the blasting knowledge that there could be no rest, no lull of oblivion for me even there. Intelligence of this presented itself in the only way that could have returned me to action. I felt a break in the spell of my gaze. Raising my head, I looked directly across into the face of Major Brent.

Masked by cedar bushes, his eyes hung before me like rotten berries, reflecting the depths from which I had just turned away. I am not sure even now whether his gaze had been fixed there for my undoing, tricking me within the radius of its transfiguring power. I say I am not sure, and I am not; but I rather think it had to do with the completed act. Unless his cunning had achieved an enlargement of pattern so far unknown to my experience with him, I had surprised him considering not me but the ruin of his youthful victim. Triumph of a sort he showed, even though it was no more than the growl of the beast over his kill. Indeed, he had the look of one who has eaten the very vitals of his victim. But the fullness of my surprise was that I now saw in him a much younger apparition, as one who had truly eaten of life. The lips pouted in a sensuous curve; there was a glow on his features; but the face, the color of that brown which none resists, showed also the mark of his torment. And it was this—equal pull between the need and the suffering it made—which contained the secret of his appeal. But the horror which fixed me there evolved from the knowledge that he could both show and disguise damnation.

So I felt as I looked up and through the cedars confronted my enemy. Perhaps I should have called out, defied him. But would this have freed me from the festering curse which poisoned my life? It might have brought me temporary relief, but the need for it was stifled in what I can remember only as a heightening of the tension. My vision had sharpened. There was no satiety on those lips: they still hungered. I had scarcely taken this in when he turned his head in a restless start. Then he was gone, gone in the very act of turning, but not before I had caught the full force of his purpose, a purpose the intent of which, if he had spoken aloud, could have been no more plainly told.

CHAPTER TWENTY-FOUR

SOMEHOW I found my way out of the woods and back to the house. I remember half running into the yard, then a deliberate slowing to a walk. I thought: it is unseemly in me to be running: I shall bring forth questions which I cannot, or had better not, at this time answer.

I felt relief at touching base again, with what had happened in the woods behind me. Then it came to me why I had hurried: Ellen. What should I tell her? I had to decide, even as I wondered how she would receive me after the night's violence, so fresh to her, so remote now to me.

The house for the first time in months was a great comfort: its lines so sure, so firm. As I walked toward it, I almost sighed with relief and gratitude for its foursquareness. There it was. Ellen would be safe within. Tears suddenly blurred my vision, and now in the late morning light all my fears seemed groundless. But this elation was momentary because the facts were hard. I had first to make my peace with Ellen; and I would, of course, now have to tell her about Moss, even to the dark end he made. My story would bring the whole thing into the open. This were better so. So

155

great a shock might break the enchantment. And besides there was no way to keep my knowledge secret. In the end the Army was sure to trace Moss. There would be questions. What ugly suspicions would not any silence of mine give rise to? Who would believe the truth? The state does not recognize ghosts. It will demand some reasonable explanation. If none is forthcoming . . .

Clammy sweat broke out on my forehead at the realization of the predicament my enemy had brought me to. I stepped quickly into the great hall and leaned my back against the shut door. For the first time I gave myself up to that low impulse, the instinctive fear only the trapped know.

Self-absorption stops all clocks, but after a while it came to me that the house did not seem the same as I had left it. At first it was no more than a vague disquietude, no more than the embarrassment one feels on discovering the change in old familiarity. And then I noticed—my consciousness was all alert now—the peculiar quality of silence the hall made. I called Ellen's name and, not waiting for an answer, rushed upstairs. She was not there. I quickly thought of the kitchen.

Maybelle was at the sink, her brown hands idling in the dishwater. She did not look up as I came in, and I knew that things were very wrong. I asked, "Where is Miss Ellen?"

"She gone off."

"Where?"

"She gone off in the car," she replied after a pause,

which I knew was a rebuke for my tone of voice.

"Did she say where she was going?" I tried to make my voice sound casual, but I knew it was useless. Maybelle knew that Miss Ellen never went off in the car by herself.

"She didn' say."

I had to get it out. "Was she alone?"

Some way, without turning her head, she managed to shift her eyes quickly toward mine; then drop them to her hands resting quietly in the greasy water. "I never seen nobody," she replied, looking through the little window at her head.

By now I was desperate. I blurted out, "Did she say when she would be back?"

"She never say."

Dreamily Maybelle picked up the dishrag and twisted it.

"Thank you," I said and turned to get out of the kitchen quickly.

At the door her voice stopped me. "She never give out no dinner. What you wants me to have?"

I stopped, at what tremendous effort of will only I will know. I collected myself to speak calmly, to give some illusion of order to this crumbling world. "Oh, bread, meat, whatever you have."

"Ain' no meat."

"Then anything you have in the house." Before I went out, I had control enough to say, "Bring a cup of coffee to my study, please."

I did not go at once to the study. I wandered aimlessly, if wander describes what I did. To wander presupposes some degree of will. Shall I say, because I breathed, because my heart still sent the blood back and forth through my body, my feet moved, but with no purpose or direction? I must have passed through every room in the house, seeing without seeing, everywhere through surroundings once familiar, now merely nonexisting. I seem to remember saying, Ellen gone—saying it; pausing; saying it again, hoping to induce some sort of response. But it was no use. Nature's kind anesthesia had deadened my senses.

I became aware of a growing restlessness, and then I saw that I was in our bedroom. Here, if anywhere, I would feel her presence. This was her creation. There was not a thing in it that had not grown in the loveliness of her eye, or been touched by her hand. But I looked around at a strange place. The curtains hung stiff and cold. The chairs sat about on display. I looked hard at the bed, thinking memory would at least restore that to meaning. But I could see only the craftsman's design as he must have seen it in the moment of intuition. There was no history for me here. Quickly I turned toward my study. There the human presence would have left its mark. Only in such a place could I recover my identity.

The cup of coffee was on the desk. It was cold, but I drank it down. With it came release and realization of the desperate pass I had reached. Moss first, and now Ellen. She had seized the moment, oh how well planned, step by cunning step, and had gone to him.

And I was helpless in this desertion, not knowing where or what even to do. Bound hand and foot and thrown into the ash heap.

Well, let her go to him. It's what she's wanted, to try the multiplicity of those dark practices his ghostly whisper set her longing for. How the old one must feel his triumph! For it was through me that she had gone to him, through me that he would at last and forever possess her. I had not been able to stand the strain. I had weakened and blundered, and he had known all along that I would! It was his way of showing his contempt for me. Oh, it was a nice, refined cruelty, this self-punishment he had devised, the black gloom of remorse and manhood's inadequacy!

I was a long time in this state. There was no pain. It was all pure suffering, a long suffocation like drowning, except that I was denied the sweet release into unconsciousness which drowning allows. And at last, when I thought I could stand no more, there began the slow dark pressure against the heart. The despondency this made is not for words to relate. Then suddenly the moment of ecstasy. When that passed, I felt as light as down, forever freed of my burden. I had done my best. I could do no more. I had nothing more to do. I could set out tomorrow, even now, on the big road and go until I dropped, with no thought but of what the day would bring and not much of that. And at night sink into sleep, sleep without dreams, and wake up with the sun as fresh as a child on the first day.

Naturally this sense of absolute freedom could not

last. I knew there was more to come. Perhaps it was the shock of looking up and finding the day almost spent that brought me back to reality. Perhaps the door made a noise as it opened. The two things came so close together I cannot even now separate them in my mind, for before I could measure the consequences of the lost time, my eyes shifted and there, just inside the threshold, stood Ellen.

She stood with perfect calm, the door half open, and looked at me. I saw at once that she was no longer innocent. There was a surety of new power about her, a mysterious experience I could never share. I got all of this on the instant, and it was plain that she remembered the night's violence even as little as I. At the least she did not draw it between us like a curtain. She regarded me in a kind of puzzlement and her eyes were large with sympathy. What arrested me was the nature of this sympathy. It was not personal, but such as one, at moments of stress, might feel for all humankind. The pause during which we regarded each other lengthened. Perhaps she was waiting for me to question her. I was trembling too much to speak. Then she said with studied restraint, "I have bad news for you."

My heart lurched. I mumbled, "Yes?"

"I've been to town."

She waited, carefully examining my face to see if her statement held special meaning for me.

I said, "Yes?"

Carefully, as if she feared the words might not carry, she said, "Moss is dead."

I leaped up. "How did you know?"

My mouth was dry. The words at first did not come out. They spluttered, cracked and broke up.

She came forward calmly and sat me in my chair. "You are overwrought," she said.

I worked my mouth. A little moisture returned. I flung at her, "Of course, you know he is dead. You knew it even before I. It is now the most simple of the sorrows you will engage."

Nothing could shatter her calm. "Of course I knew it before you. The notification came while I was at your brother's. I am late because I stayed to help."

"My brother? How could he know?"

"The Army notified him."

"The Army," I leaped up, screaming.

"Yes, Henry," she replied. "The Army. Moss has been dead three months."

CHAPTER TWENTY-FIVE

*T*HERE comes a moment in excessive strain when the body out of the economy of its mechanism, withdraws from the demands of the mind. My own had reached such a pass. It refused to send along the thin threads of the nerves any further shock. As I stood there, my flesh shut up in a self-protective paralysis, it must have seemed to Ellen that my grief was at the least extravagant.

She could have thought of it only as grief I now know. I tried to act as she thought I should act. It was in such a way I discovered the body's revolt. And the mind's endless energy. Released, it ran like an engine idling at high speed. But away from its proper vehicle.

A few simple words and a situation desperate beyond remedy had suddenly bettered itself. Indeed, would not the entire grounds for alarm have to be reassessed?

And I? What was I? How had I known Major Brent for what he was and been deluded as to Moss? Was it that the humors of matter still besmirched his spirit? While Major Brent had worn as thin as the air he inhabited? Or had I second sight? Did the

162

veil at birth hide from me the intrusion of common things? Was I set apart to suffer the visions of phantoms sifting through this veil, warped of breath, woofed so fine the spider's glue, beside it, would twine as gross as hemp?

I was not so mad as to think I was done with Major Brent. A presence of such formidable proportions would not frequent the scene of its mortal life without some dreadful purpose. I held to this and to the feeling, irrational, unprovable, that somehow Moss had interfered, perhaps even to stay its execution. I felt hope, the bright gleam of it flashing in the whirl of my mind. But things were none too clear. Perhaps it was given me to understand this purpose but to remain tongue-tied. To savor the saving words but feel them dry up overnight like a cut flower. To fail.

To fail because we, the sensible inheritors, will not face the need for any such return. When we admit the possibility, and it is always with cowardly reservations, in our earth-bound blindness we see no farther than some sentimental explanation. This is our pitiful limitation. We cannot comprehend life out of time or without matter; yet we believe in it. We are attracted to and repelled by it. Witness the desperate need to come to grips with, to explain it, to take comfort from our fear of it, which is the fabric of all religious experience and the source of the great entelechies of philosophy and the ritual of churches.

But always the vocabulary fails. We have words: spirit, soul, life after death. We have myths: fallen angels, gardens of Paradise, the resurrection of the body . . . Yet what are these but material definitions made by the senses recoiling from timely limits and from the corruption of the body into which, at last, they must disappear? How can we, fastened to and made dizzy by the turning of the earth, see but as the drunkard sees or speak other than with a thick tongue?

Prolonging the period of shock, so that some way I might readjust myself to Ellen, I wondered . . . had I blundered upon the mystery of mysteries? And why was it I who must be drawn into the expanse of this passionate emptiness, fragmentary memories of which all men guard in the back closets of their minds, not knowing the meaning but only that there is meaning, as simple tribesmen perform acts of ritual about the shards of their past, with no memory of why or what they propitiate? I can only speak, like my brothers, with the tongue of matter. I therefore speak falsely even as I report the violent secret of the gods. Or if not that secret, then the shadow of the tension on the horizon.

Ellen came over to me. "You must take hold of yourself," she said gently, touching my arm.

"Yes, yes, of course," I said.

"Come on. A little food will do us good. Let's go down, have a drink, and get supper."

With a new assurance she took me in charge and I moved in the tow of her energy like a child. We went down the back way to the kitchen. Briskly she put on her apron. I shook up the fire in the stove and soon had it going. She must have been tired from a too-full day, but she went about getting the meal as if we were playing at house.

"You poor dear," she said, looking into the warmer. "You didn't eat your dinner. You must be starved."

"I was worried about you," I answered, looking at the potatoes lying in their shriveled skins, the fried onions limp and draining grease. But it was the odor of the thick bread, from which one triangular piece had been cut away, which made me withdraw; and for a moment it seemed to cast about Ellen's efforts a cheerless miasma, that smell of frostbite leftover potatoes have and the too-heavy soakings of warm grease.

She said, "Maybelle knows better than to make that kind of bread. I shall certainly speak to her in the morning."

I said, "What made you go to town?"

She seemed not to hear my question. I was aware in the click of her heels, the pause before the icebox that she had heard me. She said, "Fix me that drink, will you? And then separate these eggs."

I quickly had the drinks made. We touched glasses and fingers. *"Prosit,"* she said and smiled. Her eyes became grave and she leaned forward and kissed me. "Darling, I know what a terrible shock it is. Moss was so fond of you. And you much more than an uncle to him." She added softly, "But you will be comforted."

"There are things I must ask you," I said. "Things I don't understand."

"I know, darling." And then, "You must go in to see your brother tomorrow. He is taking it hard, too hard. I think I felt sorrier for him than for Madge. After all, women can stand these things better."

Briskly changing her tone, "Now if you'll do the eggs and wash the lettuce. Oh, it's in the car. Will you bring my things in?"

I stepped out of the dark hall into the lesser darkness of the night. The stars were out, the sky was clear. I watched the flickering patches of light, so cold and bright, and for all the eyes that had sought them, terrifyingly remote, forever removed from human involvements. I shivered. There was a chill to the air, the first warning of winter. I took a deep breath and went to the car and picked up the bags of groceries. As I turned, I saw a dark shape waiting at the side of the drive.

"Who's that?" I asked sharply and leaned against the car to brace myself.

The figure moved forward, hesitantly but surely. "It's me, Boss."

"You, Johnny?" I had raised my voice out of the need to control it.

"You needs help?"

"No, no," I said. "I can manage."

He did not go away but remained where he was, and I where I was, with my back against the car. I let him wait, for I knew what he was here to find out. I

166

let him wait, waiting myself, now that I had to phrase
it, for an intuitive grasp at meaning. At last I said,
and my own voice surprised me, remote, apart from
me, as though it spoke out of the air and the air's dis-
tances had brought it from some far region of truth.
"I went into the woods, and you would not follow. I
went because I knew that I would find there some
clearer meaning, and I thought that I had a part and
that that part was to dispel the encroaching return of
evil. Its rapid advance I had witnessed, but I could
not define it. I knew the time was fast running out.
And this was all I knew. The danger I sensed; I did
not assess it. I lost my way and later found that the
lost way was the right way. I saw my nephew Moss;
I saw the pit into which he had gone; I saw the one
who had drawn him there. And then I came to the
house."

After a pause Johnny asked, "Mister Moss daid?"

"Yes," I replied, and my irony reached into the
night. "But he did not die at *The Grove*."

A slight movement of the immobile figure told me
the effect my words had had.

"No. No, he died three months ago, miles away,
across the waters." I felt the pure clarity of the words
as they slipped across the night.

"You say you seen him at the pit?"

Momentarily Johnny had lost his composure.

"Going toward it."

I waited, for what I was not quite sure, for some
discovery he had withheld, an apology for his equivo-

cal actions, but he quickly recovered himself. He said, "A mile don't mean nothen to a dead man."

"But he's been here. I saw him." Then I snapped, "Didn't you?"

I could hear my breath coming quick as I waited. He could not evade this question. Had I not brought him to the study where Moss was? Had I not given Moss into his care? My voice insisted, "Didn't you?"

The night seemed to grow darker, or did my eyes film, straining to see across the dividing space between us, leaning into it, to trap some expression, some disclosing movement of his body. But he receded. His powerful figure withdrew as into a murky fog. But his voice was not lost. It spoke in the formal courtesy I had come to learn as the barrier I could not breach. "No, sir," he said. "I never seen him."

"You never saw him?"

In my anger for the thing slipping away I stepped forward. I saw him plainly now, not a yard away, face me with his habitual dignity. And the smooth, silky tones, "Yes, sir. You brought me to yore room. You tole me he war there. It warn't my place to dispute you. No, sir. But I never seen him myself."

"But the food you took him?"

"I throwed hit to the chickens."

"But the bed you made?"

"I never made hit but oncet."

I was close to him now, close enough to see the sweat bead on his forehead, and his eyes roll. Then I said right into his face, "Well, what was he doing here? Why did I think it was my nephew? And he all the time dead somewhere in the Pacific."

Johnny stepped back a step. He said very quietly, "Maybe he come here to tell you sump'm. Maybe he done tole you, kin you cipher hit."

My gaze must have wandered, for as I looked into the darkness to question him further, he was gone.

And then I heard Ellen's voice. "Where are you, dear?"

I saw that I had dropped the bundles. I picked them up and went slowly toward the back kitchen door.

CHAPTER TWENTY-SIX

I COULD see alarm spread from the corner of her eye, but she made the error of trying to cover it up. As I set the bundles down, she said, "You need a haircut. And a bath. You mustn't let yourself go because we live in the country. It makes you look, oh look so weird. I know now why the English colonials make such a ritual of the toilet."

"They are bored," I said.

"What made you so long? I was beginning to be worried."

"I ran into Johnny," I said casually. At least I had meant to be casual.

"At this time of night? What did he want? Anything wrong?"

"No. Just the usual thing."

She knew I was lying. Her manner became brisk again. "Well, supper is nearly ready. As soon as I put the meat on and make the bread. You can do the salad and I'll be ready to pull it together." She was kneeling at the flour bin. "I've poured you another drink. It's on the table."

"I hadn't finished the first one," I said.

"Oh," she replied. "Well, let's make it a loving cup."

"Let's," I said.

I took a long drink from mine and felt the hot sting at the bottom of my stomach. And then quickly I set to work. My hands broke the leaves from the lettuce head and I tossed them into a pan of cold water. I washed and picked the cress; threw in several leaves of the darker spinach; put some eggs on to boil. I took another drink. I began to feel better, much better, restored now as the spirits entered my blood and followed its intricate pattern into the veins. "It's wonderful what whisky can do for you," I said.

"You needed it, darling. You looked dreadfully undone."

"And you looked tired."

"Yes, I've had rather a day of it."

"What made you run into town? You must have made up your mind in a hurry."

"I did rather. Let's not go into it now."

"It's almost as if you knew . . ."

She turned to me. For the first time she seemed a little shaken.

"It is eerie," she said.

"You mean Moss?"

"Oh, the whole thing."

She broke off. Her voice resumed its light conversation tone. "I bought some tomatoes. They looked good for so late in the season."

"Maybe I'd better marinate them," I said. "Where are they?"

171

"In the top of that sack on the table. The small sack."

I reached down and brought them out, three large beautiful red tomatoes. I could tell they were solid meat through to the heart, with no hard green core, but perhaps a little ripe—so that they would leak around the seed.

"These ought to be drained first, shouldn't they?"

I held one up. It was almost ready to burst with ripeness.

"It's easy to see why they were called love apples," I said.

"The old people thought to eat them was to die, I've heard," she said.

"Do you suppose they made the connection?"

"Love sometimes kills," Ellen answered me gently.

I sensed that she had paused and that she had spoken out of some inner fear and that she was unaware that she had spoken. Not since her return, since the stroke of her news, had I felt so near to the rending of the veil which hid us from the truth. But how could I get her to tell me precisely what she feared?

I prompted: "There's an older truth about love and death."

"Well, I don't want to hear it. Not tonight anyway."

For a while after this the kitchen was silent, except for the light familiar sounds we made at our separate jobs. Into this silence gradually came, almost as if invoked, the feeling of communion as we went about

the common meal together. I was ravenously hungry,
I who had felt no appetite all day, and the smell of
food, its promise of restoration, took on a tremendous
significance. For a moment my exhausting vigil seemed
as remote as some old fable lingering on in the mind
from childhood. I went over to Ellen and put my arms
around her and we kissed as we had not kissed for a
long time. No words passed; there was no need for
words, those props to faulty communication.

I released her and she began to make up the bread.
It seemed right that she should pass from my embrace
to this, for her movements were a ritual as old as the
world. A little frown shaded her eyes, her arms rose
and fell in effortless rhythm, her hands seemed to pun-
ish and caress the flesh-colored dough. My eye followed the next step in observation: the dough was
flesh-colored but it was not the color of life. My
nerves were still inflamed. I stepped back a little from
the biscuit block, for surely now I saw the meaning
of Ellen's motion: she did the things with her hands
one does to bring life back to the body of the drowned.
Unaware that I had withdrawn, as though she still
felt me there participating, she rolled the bread to the
proper thickness and then took her biscuit cutter and
with quick wrist motions cut the dough, lifting the
small round pieces into the pan.

"Open the oven door, will you?" she said.

Her request had the sound of words, any words,
which may be spoken but whose meaning only the initi-
ate can understand.

173

The heat blew into our faces. As she leaned forward, her eyes glistened. Slowly she shoved the pan into the oven's mouth and I, as if the time had come to play my part, lifted the door until it clicked to with finality.

We stood by the stove a moment.

"I do hope they will rise," she said.

"Well, let's drink to the resurrection," I replied.

"Don't be sacrilegious, darling." She shuddered slightly. "It's bad luck."

I looked for our glasses. They were empty. "We're down to the loving cup," I said.

I held the tumbler toward her; her hands were dusty with flour.

She drank, and then I drank.

"You'd better hurry with your salad, dear. It won't be long now."

I rubbed the garlic until its strength hovered at the bowl's mouth, and then I picked up the lettuce, wonderfully fresh and crisp. I began to dry it.

"I'll declare, the water has done a lot for this."

"I know," she said. "It wasn't very good, but it was the best I could find. You don't get good lettuce out of stores. We must try to grow fall lettuce in the garden."

"The sun would burn it up."

"I wonder why," she sighed, "it will only grow well in the spring of the year?"

"I've told you. It's all greenness and water. It can't

174

stand the sun. It's a plant that goes to seed quickly. There are people like that."

She caught my eyes, saw where the suggestion had led me, and said very softly, "Like . . ."

"I suppose. Like Moss."

We hung on the vast abyss his name made, when I deliberately broke the mood. I reached for the loving cup and handed it to her. "Let's drink to Moss," I said.

"All right, darling. Let's."

She raised the tumbler and held it before her for a moment with both hands. The light had struck the heavy glass and made a thin stream of fire in the amber liquid, so that it seemed to take on life from Ellen's hands. And then it came to me, looking at her with that clarity which can only be the focus of the true vision that I was in the presence of beauty which men of all time have been unable to resist, whose grace drives mad or leads to salvation—a grace impossible therefore miraculous, of incorruptible innocence and voluptuous play inexhaustible, the immortal heart spending and restoring at the same stroke.

"To our Moss!" she said. The shadow returned to her eyes. She sipped the drink and then passed the tumbler to me.

I grasped it.

"To Moss who will never die!"

And then I drained the glass. We faced each other and did not move.

"You are smiling?" she said.

"It's nothing. The most curious thing. Something completely irrelevant just popped into my head."

"But what?"

"I'm ashamed. I don't understand."

"I want to know."

"I was thinking of Jim. A colored boy on the home place."

"But?"

"What has it to do with Moss? Nothing. Absolutely nothing."

"Well," she said, "what about Jim?"

"Once at communion, when the chalice passed, he turned it up as I did just now and drank it down. He said, 'I love my Jesus so much, I'm goen drink him all up.'"

"Darling," Ellen said firmly, "what you need is food. And plenty of it. Get busy with that salad."

And I did, and she got busy. The light tap of her heels, the low clatter of dishes, her quick movements from kitchen to dining room, the ordered array of table gear, the last minute's seasoning—all of this, bending over the salad bowl, I half saw, half heard. From dish to dish, from table to oven, back and forth, she was now lost in that last act of pulling the meal together. I waited, expectant; and then squeezed from mouth to stomach, I took the blind spasm and the whirl, the afterfaintness, the swallow, and knew that only food could save me from passing out. Concentrating, I walked a quick step to the dining room with the salad.

The silver, the china, the bottle of wine, were in place, pure and shining, with the air of expectancy and the promise of fulfillment which the board takes on before one sits down to eat. Very carefully I walked back to the kitchen. In the bread boat Ellen was laying out the white napkin.

I waited. She opened the oven door. "The bread is done," she said.

"Good. I can't wait much longer."

"Here," she commanded. "Take these dishes in and be sure to put them on the pads."

I then brought the meat and put it before me. I stood, waiting for her; and she entered, bringing the bread boat, with the napkin folded three ways over the biscuit. She set it to her right and then took her seat.

"Now we can begin," she said and a sigh passed her lips.

I made a quick blessing and began to carve. The plates passed back and forth. In reverent tones of praise I said, "What wonderful food!"

"Thank you, love."

We did not speak again until the pangs of hunger had been appeased, sighing and sitting back in our chairs.

"I've got to catch my breath," I said.

"And I. My, but I was starved."

"I never saw you eat so," I said in a teasing way.

"I never had such need before."

At that moment, looking across the board now in

177

such disarray, above the crumbs, the bits of food, the stains on the white cloth, above the dishes our appetites had emptied, Ellen and I at the same instant caught each other's eye and smiled. It was a secret smile, perfect in its sympathy, almost perfect in its understanding. I knew at last that spiritual unity which is the end of marriage. And I knew that I might now speak and she would understand.

But she spoke first, a little sadly but with no false sentiment. She said, "One would think we had forgotten Moss. But we needed this. Particularly you, darling, to help you bear up in your sorrow and the greatness of your disappointment. You thought of him as your heir. Thoughts of him have made us feel justified in our struggle with this old place."

"Helen," I said abruptly, "his death is our salvation. I am going to take you away from *The Grove*. The place is haunted. We will be haunted if we stay."

"Darling, you called me Helen."

"My tongue must be a little thick."

"You almost drank too much."

"Yes," I said with awe which I hardly understood, "I almost did. But I am sober now. We are going to clear out of here. And tomorrow."

"Perhaps," she replied and the resonance of her voice made me tremble, "perhaps you will change your mind."

"It's made up," I replied, but the words died away.

"I have other news for you," she said, dropping her eyes to look up quickly and frankly.

"Yes," I whispered, sitting straight in the chair, sensing that from her lips would come the confession which would free or forever bind us to whatever fatal entanglements I had involved us in. Wild, mad thoughts raced through my mind as I endured the pause she made; but wild, mad, driving me beyond hope and despair, I sensed my inability to foresee.

"Yes," I said again, and my voice must have told her how unbearable was my suspense, for she said quickly, but in a voice so low that I thought I had mistook it:

"I am going to have a baby."

I suppose I merely sat without expression, without sign of any intelligence on my face. She hurried on, "I know we'd thought this couldn't be. But I've suspected it for some time. And the doctor assures me it is so." And then, as I still sat motionless, without response, she added, "The child will come in the spring."

CHAPTER TWENTY-SEVEN

*I*T WAS nothing less than a miracle: that a chronic sterility should suddenly disappear without reason or possible explanation, and furthermore at *The Grove* which I had hoped to regenerate, thinking less of myself than of a larger pattern, although naturally I made a part of that pattern. After the surprise, the moment of unbelievable elation, the coincidence began to seem a little too pat. A miracle, of course, is a miracle. It is not to be explained. One explains the unexplainable by calling it a miracle. One does not really expect to witness it. And there was no other way to regard our prospect of an heir. If we had deliberately denied ourselves a child, later to reverse our decision . . . even then we might have expected a reluctant nature to deal with. But this—it was a bolt from the blue.

It came to me, not at first of course, but gradually and much later, that the changed status represented possibilities which I at first in no way even glimpsed. I could not have been expected to see beyond the fact, and a fact above all of such exciting vistas. At the moment it answered everything. It dispelled all my suspicions as to Ellen's communication with the sinister specter which haunted our lives, for obviously a pregnant woman is strange. Obviously she has had communication with the mysterious workings of life which a man cannot comprehend, and which certainly I, given my absorption with another mystery, equally insoluble, was in no way prepared to suspect.

But also it gave me a firm answer to what had come to seem an irresponsible, a romantic, act. Now I knew that my good Daemon had deliberately led me to *The Grove*. Not to escape the accident of the world but to come into my own. I was now to be the head of a family, a true family, returned to my proper place, and that place physically and spiritually of a sound and explicable history.

I remained in this condition of elation for what was left of the fall season. We did not have that year a slow dying away into winter. The last of September was crisper than usual; it was even cold. And by early October we had had a light frost. Johnny had told me that the shucks were thick on the corn. I knew what that meant—a long hard winter. As time approached when the tobacco had to be cut, I had mighty little time for thinking. It rained a good deal, and when it didn't rain the days were cloudy. That worry which comes from the prospect of losing the year's work, of not paying taxes or the interest on the mortgage, began to creep through the farm. Every time we would meet we would tell ourselves that there was plenty of time. We would look at the tobacco, a fair enough crop, and say to each other there is plenty of time. And then we would look at the overcast sky. You've got to have sun when it's cut to make the leaves fall, or you can't put it on the sticks.

From the moment I took the lead I found the tension exhilarating. Formerly, emergencies and crises had filled me with the nameless fears that come from an inability to act. But this had passed. I found I had a real interest in what was going on. I found I could act. I had that sense of holding things in the palm of my hands; and it was due to my management that the tobacco was cut and hung in the barns three days before the killing frost. My neighbors were not, all of them, so successful. A few lost the great part of their crops, many too great a fraction. My reputation among these hardheaded people reached a height which certainly I and more certainly they had never expected. Even Johnny showed me greater deference. There was no marked change in his attitude, but he would ask my advice on little things, even on matters he understood better than I. Somehow I felt that the life of the place, for decades submerged deep within the ground, stirred again and slowly was groping through the hard-packed soil to air and light.

As Johnny and I parted one evening at dusk—we had been discussing the farm's luck—he turned to me and said, "Folks says you talks to the devil."

"Why, what on earth do they mean?"

The shadows of the night were rushing fast about us, so that I could not well see his eyes, but for an instant I was aware that they no longer regarded me from their habitual reticence. They fixed upon me an intimate, almost conspiratorial gleam. It quickly died. He said, "Hit puzzles them how you done it."

"It ought not to," I said, a little annoyed without knowing why. "They've cut and hauled enough tobacco to know how it is done."

"Yessir, that's the p'int," he replied softly.

I could get no more out of him. Nor was it necessary, for the drift of his remark was clear. What was not clear was why he felt it necessary to inform me.

I repeated the conversation to Ellen. She looked at me very strangely, which also caused me to wonder. She was already beginning to show, as they say, and her face was changing somewhat; so it may have been nothing more than her condition. And certainly her reply was very sensible. "I wouldn't pay any attention to that," she said. "You know how envious country-people are."

I hadn't really paid any attention to it, not to take it seriously, that is, until Ellen advised me not to. I realized then that it had worried me a little, or rather that a grain of anxiety lay far back in my head and this incident had jolted it to the fore. Soon after we went in to supper and after supper sat down in our common living room and she and I began to talk about one thing and another. I remember hearing my brother's name mentioned and then sometime after Ellen saying, "You are not listening."

"But I am. You were talking about Moss Senior and Madge."

"I was saying," she answered with annoyance, "the stone they want for Moss's grave is too ornate. And it is rushing things so. It will be months before his body is brought back."

"I must have dozed off."

"Go to bed then."

I stood up to go. "I'll check the fires in the barns first," I said.

I heard her voice, waveringly, as from a distance, "Well, go ahead. Don't stand there in the middle of the floor."

"I'm going."

Once outside the night air braced me and I could think clearly again. I was absolutely sure I had got up to go to bed. I had had no intention of going to the barns. Johnny would be there, or if not there, he would have checked the fires and left one of his sons in charge if he thought there was any need for it. I had stood up, opened my mouth to yawn—I was sure of this—and the words came out. They were not my words. No . . . they were not my words, but they were meant for me . . .

A light wind had come up and blew the wood smoke in the direction of the house. For some time the smell had sifted down the air like a clean, sharp spice. Now it came in heavier gusts, insistent, commanding. I began walking toward the first barn.

Even before I could see him, I knew Johnny was there. I called out, in no loud way but my voice went far, "Things all right?" And a little after I saw his shape against the large barn doors.

He did not answer until I came up. " 'Backer's still high. I picked up the fars a little."

"There's a ring around the moon," I said.

"Yessir, hit due to rain."

We were silent awhile. The night was soft. The smell from the barn, so clean and sharp, was somehow comforting. I wondered why I had felt uneasy, now that all things seemed clear at last, and right. I felt the sudden need to be confidential. We were both of us looking up at the sky. I dropped my eyes to a group of trees at the edge of the woods. The shadows there bred a stillness closer than the spaces of the sky. Looking into them, I said, *"The Grove* will have an heir sometime this spring."

I could see Johnny drop his gaze and fix it on the trees before us. Together we stared into the shadows and after an appropriate pause, he said, "You shore means to hold fast to the plow."

I don't know what I had expected, some conventional compliment, some acknowledgment which would show me he understood my fresh strength, my changed status. Perhaps I even hoped he would hint that now I deserved a son. Certainly I did not expect so ambiguous a remark and almost at once I felt a chill in the air, a desire to go, my confidence somehow betrayed. I could have kicked myself. What a fool to lay myself open in any such way! I said coolly, "I will take a look at the fires and go to bed."

Johnny did not stir. I looked at him expectantly. He said, "Hit's turrible smoky in there."

"I'll take a look anyway."

He undid the chain on the small side door with no other word, and I quickly stepped inside. I went head down into the stifling, flickering air. Almost at once my eyes began to water and the hot acrid smoke made me choke for breath. The little lips of fire, some slightly blazing, some mere red glows, lay in orderly fashion along the floor of the barn. I had never seen a barn going at night, and for one crazy moment I had the sense that the fires came out of swollen slits in the ground. I stood for a moment, breathing carefully through my nose and squinting, looking into the gloom. The four walls gave an unbearable sense of pressure, the solid tons of leaf above, the close ranks of greenish-brown blades thrusting downward their curling points, the bright points of the gleams below, driving the thin columns of smoke upward into the parting leaves, the darkness shifting, whirling in the reddish haze. My head began to whirl. Johnny wandered noiselessly through the smoke, reaching up, feeling, gently touching a leaf here, a leaf there. Once he turned my way. His eyes were open and set in a steady gaze. I reached up and fingered the crisp twist in the moist leaf.

And then I heard it, we both heard it at the same moment. We both turned at the same moment. There came a slight puff from the center of the barn, a few sparks, and a chunk breaking in two. My eyes were stinging, but they dried up at what they saw: the figure of a man stooping, bent over the fire. Gently his arms began to flap like a bird's, slowly, steadily, as if he were fanning the embers. I looked more sharply and he seemed to be pushing the sawdust against the burning chunks. I could almost swear the sawdust moved. As I stared, the motion of his hands changed to a pat and a scoop, and then to a slow squeeze, as if they were gathering up something that was about to escape.

Suddenly he became very still and I knew that he was aware that he was being watched. Almost imperceptibly his head bent to an upward twist, moving through the smoke. So still was the rest of his body, I thought of a jointed manikin whose neck was being moved by invisible strings. But it was no manikin. It was my enemy, Major Brent, and again his gaze was fixed to mine. Again I had the feeling that I had taken him by surprise. His face, as red as the coals he was hovering over, distinctly carried an appeal, but it was so loathsome in its naked directness he must have seen how it repelled me. In a flash he was threatening me, and the cold fury of it left me shivering in the heat of the barn.

And then my eyes watered. Furiously I wiped them, but when I saw again Major Brent was nowhere. Where he had crouched, I saw only a thick column of smoke. It wavered as though something had disturbed it and then grew even, funneling steadily upward until it lost itself among the tips of the leaves.

Outside I waited for Johnny. He was leaning against the small portal. His hands with the swift, easy movement of long accustomed intimacy drew the chain through and noiselessly dropped a twig into a link. He remained for a moment pressed against the door, his head slightly bent and waiting.

I said hoarsely, "Did you see what I saw?"

It seemed a long while before he answered.

"I seen a chunk burn in two."

"And what else?"

Slowly, as one recollects the image before speaking, he said, "Hit flared, the sparks busted loose, but they ain't no harm to *them*." And then in a sudden change of tone, almost to a low rhythmic chant, "Firing a barn of tobaccer ain't the same by night. I knows what's there. I knows time I steps inside the do'. I can lay down in bed and know what's there. I knows what's in one fare and I knows what's in an'er." His voice trailed off. . . . "I don't have to see what I sees. I knows."

CHAPTER TWENTY-EIGHT

STRANGELY enough, after I had set out for the house, my first reaction was a feeling of relief. The promise of an heir for *The Grove* had taken Major Brent by surprise. At the moment when he thought to draw near his chasm of victory, his entire campaign miscarried and he disappeared from view. Not that I felt for a moment he had gone for good, but as weeks passed into months, I confess I had hopes, even if doubt burned beneath like a pilot light. Now it was flaring, in the brilliancy of its flame I saw what had happened. Major Brent had not fled: he had merely gone underground. This meant a change of tactics on his part. Failing in direct assault, if it is possible to refer to any of his methods as direct, he would now try us by surprise. Toward this end he lay in wait, and in a secret place which showed a public face. It was cunning of him but not cunning enough. I had found him out.

He had not expected me. Of this I was certain, for how else was I to interpret that appeal of his, so quickly changing into a threat? No, I was sure I had happened on a clue to his vulnerability. This gave me a feeling of self-confidence, in spite of the immense danger and everything now to lose, for who could believe other than that all his evil would turn upon the child? He must have known that I was come too late to *The Grove*. He must also have surmised that I would prepare it for our son.

In the acceptance of the changed situation I had no immediate fears for Ellen. She was not free of danger certainly; the danger was tremendously increased, but it was the kind I could face because she would face it with me. Indeed, I had now become her support, rather than she the object of my care. So it came about I did not go at once to the house but wandered over the place, questioning, trying to understand.

Gradually the truth showed itself through the confusion of half-truths, false conjectures, seemingly interminably mixed and obscure, like the shake of a puzzle when the disordered pieces fall each into its proper place and the whole is visible. The truth seemed simple enough, at least its paraphrase did. False romantic that I was when I first came with my idea, how was I to know when I bought a run-down farm to restore that I had bought nothing, that the fiction to own, in spite of deed and possession, describes the most ephemeral of all artifices? How was I to know that I had put myself in way of the past and the future, bemused by the mad fancy that I could reach into history and regenerate, a function proper only to a god? In greater humility and wisdom my idea gave way to a fuller vision of the rich complexities of circumstance and the unknowable mystery of the nature of *The Grove*. In this fuller knowledge it came to me with the suddenness of revelation: was not my idea the obverse of Major Brent's act, with the difference that he had died unrepentant and the vanity of his act bound him in torment to the shadowy air of the place, haunting it until that time he could work his release? And it was just in this that our danger lay. Unpurged, unregenerate spirit that he was, he would know only to seek his release through a repetition of the original error. But there is a blindness to phantoms. Beyond history, they think they may perpetuate it. I slapped my leg with glee as I thought of this. At least this was the conclusion I had reached that night and, once reached, the logic of warning Ellen without delay sent me toward the house.

I found her sitting up in bed, with the bedside lamp burning but with a dim flame. As I came up I saw at once the strain on her face.

"What is it?" I asked in alarm.

"Where have you been?" she demanded in a tight, injured tone. "You've been away for hours. I was about to dress and look for you."

"Is that all?" I asked with relief.

"Is that all? Is that all?" She repeated. "Leaving me to worry, not to know, lying here thinking of all the things that could happen. And in my condition."

"I'm sorry, darling, so sorry," I said softly, sitting beside her and taking her hand.

She withdrew it petulantly. "I can explain," I said hastily.

"Explain? Explain what?"

She looked up and her eyes were dark, swimming in dark pools.

It was not yet time.

I undressed and got into bed and before I could speak, she turned toward me, drawing her legs up, with her head close to mine and her hair outspread on the pillow. "Sometimes, dear, I get so afraid."

I ran my fingers carefully along her arm, barely touching the flesh and after a while I heard her sigh. And then she said, "It is only when I am tired or something makes me nervous, but I can't help thinking of those poor women. I know it is silly and that it was long ago . . ."

"Poor women?" I asked, not following.

"Yes. The women in the garden."

"Oh," I said. "Oh . . . Major Brent's wives."

"All of them died in childbed." What sorrow her voice carried as she said it, then, "I just can't get them out of my mind."

"You poor darling! They've nothing to do with you."

I drew her into my arms again. She snuggled close into my body and we lay together in the comfort of this embrace. When I felt her relax and grow quieter, I decided the time had come. I knew I must not be startling. I must in no way frighten her. And to me my voice sounded casual enough. It seemed in no way the bearer of what must have been to her strange tidings, a voice out of a dream perhaps, with the sharp

192

impersonality of a dream. . . ." I saw Major Brent tonight," I whispered.

We had reached that hour of the night when the heart sleeps, but I felt in hers a skip in the gentle fluttering, then a great lunging stroke. She stirred, drew back her head, watching me, her eyes poised on the edge of shadow made by the lamp. "What did you say?" she asked.

"I saw Major Brent tonight."

Very carefully she withdrew from my arms. Her hand had scarcely pushed away the unruly hair when her bewildered voice said, "What on earth do you mean?"

"On the earth, yes." I was sitting opposite her. "But not from gravity."

She was shaking me now. "Wake up. You are dreaming."

Carefully I placed my hands on her shoulders and lifted her around so that the light might show my face.

"Do I look as if I were dreaming?"

Her hands fluttered before her, then drew back against her breast in instant spasm. In a voice deep, harsh, choked, not hers surely, she said, "Your eyes. Your eyes," and then in a loud scream, half-animal, half-human, she leaped to the floor, where she stood trembling.

I went toward her as carefully as I could, almost creeping across the rug, for I knew the slightest jerky movement would send her off again. In fact I was so shaken by this unexpected reaction to my carefully planned attempt not to frighten that I myself was unnerved.

The distance gradually narrowed between us until I was near enough to touch her. "You must calm yourself," I said. "You have behaved out of reason." And then more forcefully, "You must think of your child."

"I must think of my child," she repeated as a child would repeat a lesson. And all the while her teeth were chattering. I waited for what seemed a long time and she said again, "I must."

"Come now," I said and gently took her by the arm. She was very docile as I led her back to bed.

CHAPTER TWENTY-NINE

*I*N THE few hours that were left to the night I tried to tell her of our danger. I went into the history of what I had seen. I tried to make clear the nature of the menace, how logically it came out of the past. At first she asked a few questions, but as I talked she gradually fell into silence, and once so still had she grown I thought she had fallen asleep. But she answered me quick enough when I questioned her. Fearing her fears, I showed her how much stronger our position had become since her pregnancy, but that in a way this was also our weakness. We must never be off guard. Nor must she ever be frightened into any rash act if Major Brent appeared to her. He was bound to await the right moment, when she would be on a stairway, or in some dangerous spot where sight of him could easily cause her to lose footing, with what disastrous consequences she could imagine. I wound up by saying, "It is your frailty or mine, some defect of ours, he will pounce upon to undo us."

I had done the best I knew to impress upon her the seriousness of the situation, but I must say I was disappointed at the way she took it. So much depended on close alliance between us, and it was just this that was

195

somehow lacking. Her disbelief—I could call it nothing else—left me for many days in a quandary. Disbelief was the last thing I had expected, for obviously our ends were the same. Our sympathy and understanding had never been closer, and so much depended on giving the child a chance. Our sanity, our very lives might depend on it. One may imagine how at a loss I was when she accused me of being cruel, by telling ghost stories when she already had enough to worry her. These were more or less her words. It was useless to insist that my intention had been anything but that. To prove it I showed her how carefully I had gone about telling her. I had been matter-of-fact, in no way making it seem strange or unnatural. No, I had kept my head. I had been in a way a scientific reporter of the menace I had witnessed; I had even tried to define the nature of the evil. And for all my pain to be accused of indulging in a cruel jest!

I think at least I had made her see that it was no jesting matter. Early in December my brother Moss Senior surprised me by coming out to see us. He had once before made a perfunctory visit, to see, as he put it, just how big a fool I had been to bury myself away from civilization. His conclusion was that I was a bigger fool than even he had imagined—which, I remarked, was indeed a large order. So, when I saw him turning up the driveway, I knew he had not returned out of a sense of pleasure or for my society.

From his manner I sensed that Ellen had communicated with him in some way, and to save her embarrass-

ment I took him walking over the place. I walked him
hard with what grim delight one may imagine; showed
him the crops in the barns, the stock in the lots, the
plans for the coming year. I showed him the good land,
the land that had to be rebuilt; I showed him the rav-
ages of the past. At last, when he was on the verge of
apoplexy I sat him down on a log to let him catch his
breath. Then I said, "Now, Brother, what did you
really come to see me about?"

He coughed, hummed and hawed, but at last came
out with it. "What is this about you seeing ghosts?"

"Did Ellen write you?"

He hesitated, in his clumsy way trying to protect her.
As if she needed protection from me! The idea was so
preposterous I laughed out right in his face. Such a
laugh would have made him angry at any other time,
but I had fairly exhausted him, and much of his old
contempt for me, which was only a part of his contempt
for mankind, had softened since his son's death. The
flesh, I noticed, hung loose on his jowls. His eyes, usually so sharp and cold, had begun to water. No, definitely he was not the man he had been. But something
of his old self came out, as he stood up. "Ghost stories
is damn poor entertainment for a pregnant woman."

I said coldly, "What did Ellen write you?"

He reached in his pocket and handed me the letter:

I have been thinking of you and Madge a great
deal lately. Now that I am going to have a child
your own sadness seems so much more real to me.
I feel so close to you now. My thoughts of the

child I am bearing, of the dangers he will encounter, of that first risk of air and light, seem all
so tremendously grave. I try to get a better perspective by telling myself how narrow are my
fears to your sorrow—the years of care and
thought, the years of fear after fear for his
safety. And then the sudden brutal news.

I suppose it is a kind of hysteria—but I often
feel that we are so far away here, that so much
could happen—it is hard to get a doctor. And then
I wonder if this undertaking hasn't been too much
for your brother. He feels so deeply—he is so
highly nervous. At first I had thought coming
here would do him good, but he told me not long
ago that he saw the ghost of old Major Brent.
He has got it into his head that it is some kind of
a threat to us, particularly to the baby—not a very
cheerful subject of conversation to me right now.

I was wondering if you could find us a place in
town, where we could go at least until the baby is
born.

I feel sometimes that a sort of doom hangs over
The Grove. Perhaps I'll be seeing ghosts too if
we spend the long winter months shut up in this
house.

I tell myself that my foreboding is only a part
of pregnancy and should not be indulged. . . .
Don't give this letter too much thought. My love
to Madge.

ELLEN.

I stood there with the letter in my hand. My poor,
poor Ellen! To what desperate plight had I brought
her that she would turn to Moss Senior? To what

desperate despair had I brought myself in so miserably failing to reach through to her? Never in my trade, where I succeeded modestly in making the illusions of life seem more real than life itself, never had I sweated as I had to present for her the true image of reality. Only to be caught, trapped behind the skill of my trade, so that she saw what only the world would see, a ghost story. I could not lay it to her condition: the failure lay elsewhere: in my style.

Major Brent—a ghost story! How that abominably monstrous spirit, hiding in air, breeding pestilence, must be chuckling at this turn of affairs! What desperate irony for me, perfecting the cry of wolf, wolf, now to be undone by perfection!

"You ought to get down on your knees to that little woman for what you have done to her," I heard; and the arrogance of the tone crossed my nerves like a file. For the next few moments I was trembling beyond control. Blind murderous flashes disordered my senses. But I took myself in hand. At last, with tremendous effort I opened my eyes.

"Let's go back to the house," he said, turning abruptly. But I saw. He did not turn quickly enough to hide his fear—of me the brother he had always held in contempt.

We did not speak again until we reached the entrance way, when I said, "Obviously it will not be good for Ellen here now. Will you find us a place in town?"

"That's more sense than you've spoken in your whole

life," he replied in a gruff surly way. And then his
true nature came to the fore even in this situation.
"Places are hard to get, but I think maybe I can put
my hands on something. You leave it up to me."

"I always do," I said.

My brother had never been one to catch even the
bluntest shadings of irony.

CHAPTER THIRTY

*A*ND so it was settled before he left for town; it was settled as the tea leaves grew cold in the bottom of the cups. We all made the best of an embarrassing situation. Even Moss Senior became civilized in a neolithic kind of way. And before he left for town, we actually set a date of departure, my brother offering us quarters with him in case he had not found us a place in the meantime. I protested this and, as it was growing late, invited him to spend the night. Ellen pressed him, but he refused. Soon thereafter, pleading bad roads and the approaching dark, he took his departure.

I could feel Ellen dreaded the moment when we would be alone and we both must face her going behind my back. I did not tell her that Moss Senior had abused her confidence and showed me the letter, for I was determined there was to be no further rift in our understanding. Whatever the failure it was mine, since it had been up to me to communicate. I told her quite frankly that I understood, that she must forgive me, that what I knew I knew, that I had acted for the best, and that for a long time now fleeing *The Grove* had not crossed my mind. I at last was beginning to

201

feel at home here, at last the responsible head and equal
to my responsibility. What I had not realized was her
own fresh alarm, but I told her that I understood her
difficulties of belief and thoroughly agreed that what
she wanted was best, that above all we must think of
her and the special meaning her pregnancy held for us
both. She was very relieved and, I think, surprised.
She kissed me and said, "Oh, I am so glad you understand."

"I do," I said. "But I must tell you I am not a patho-
logical case."

She interrupted me quickly. "Of course not, Henry."

I went on. "There is more around us than the natural world."

"Of course," she said.

"I am more than your natural husband."

The sweet sincerity of her reply moves me now, as
it did then, with all the fresh pity I felt for her and for
myself as she put her hands lightly on my shoulders
and said, "You are the father of my child."

I know I was close to tears, for I had to take her and
hold her tight, as much to gain control of myself as to
comfort her. But I could not indulge in the weakness
of feeling: I must be honest with her and with myself.
So I said, "But, Ellen dear, you must believe me. I am
not superstitious. I am not what you may have thought.
I was never stronger. There is an evil influence here.
That influence I have met and met again. It is a threat
to us. It will not go until I make it go."

She thought a long while before she spoke again.

Her words were quietly given, I could see she was struggling to understand. "How can you be sure?" she asked.

"How can you be sure of those tea-things there?"

"Why, they are there," she said.

"Exactly. And Major Brent is there"—I waved my hand toward the outside.

She lifted an empty cup. "This I can see, touch. Can you touch Major Brent?"

I put my hand on her stomach. She withdrew slightly; then became still, almost poised for flight. We both felt it, I the swelling movement roll within her. She looked at me. "He just kicked," she said.

"I felt him," I said.

Almost desperately she replied, "Don't you see? He is real. He is important."

"He is." I paused to give my words effect. "But can you see him?"

"Of course not. But he is no less real for that."

"Exactly. We do not need all our senses. One is enough sometimes. I have not touched, but I have seen Major Brent."

"But how can you know? You don't know what he looks like."

"But Johnny does."

"Johnny!" She threw his name at me in contempt.

"The descriptions match," I went on.

She turned away and began piling the tea-things on the tray. There was nothing but the soft clatter of dishes and tinkle of silver. Suddenly she looked up.

"All right. But then I must go to town. It is not right to make this child suffer any risk, whatever it is."

"I've agreed."

This seemed to calm her. And I let it go at that and considered that it came off well. What use to tell her that nothing could be gained by moving to town? Was not the air everywhere familiar to Major Brent? For us to leave *The Grove* would only be to make us more vulnerable. To remove ourselves would in no way throw Major Brent off the scent. It would only place us in strange surroundings.

There was one thing sure in all of this: my brother. He acted true to form. With his usual lack of consideration for others, he transferred one of his keymen to another town so that we could have his house. Of course even Moss Senior could not throw the man into the streets without warning, the upshot being we could not get the house until the first of the year. In the meanwhile we were told in lordly fashion we could move in with our kinsman. But this I refused to do, and Ellen seemed content to stay on at *The Grove* until we could get the house. I made it clear that, if she wished, we would go to the local hotel in the interim. My thorough willingness to do anything she proposed, I think, made Ellen feel she was being somewhat of an alarmist and she hurriedly agreed the thing to do was to stay on at *The Grove* until the first of the year.

Even the weather seemed to conspire to keep us there. The days were mild and moist, with brisk chilly nights. It was perfect tobacco weather, and the crops were all got down and bulked and by Christmas a good part of it was stripped. We spent a quiet Christmas, thinking how different the next one would be. The rest of December went quickly, Ellen busy with the packing, and I in straightening out my accounts. We had set the following Monday to leave. On Friday the worst blizzard the country had known for twenty years blew out of the northwest. It began with a heavy downpouring rain, a regular gully-washer which lasted ten hours, when the wind changed and turned a slow drizzle into sleet. The temperature dropped twenty degrees in five hours. By the next morning the snow was deep on the ground and still falling. We stood together at our bedroom window and looked out on the wintry world. Hesitantly I said, "This will delay us. The roads are solid ice."

Ellen was so long making any kind of response I naturally turned her way. She was staring . . . well, she was staring into the frozen outdoors with such dismay, her shoulders drawn in and so pitifully thin and her eyes, all their luster gone, protruding in the set way of a doll's made for a melodramatic role. "This won't last long," I said heartily. "It never does in this country."

"I was afraid of this," she said. She repeated the words several times with desperate earnestness, as if she saw the proof of some truth she alone had been sure of. I touched her arm. "Come now. It's not all that bad."

"I won't be able to leave," she said.

"I promise you. Now make us some tea."

As it happened, I was a poor weather prophet.

Each day the thermometer dropped a degree or two. When the sun came out, and this was not every day, it would rise for a little and then sluggishly drop to its previous reading, or below it. The cattle stood hunched up in the barn lot, or picking at the frozen wisps of hay half sunk in the frozen mass about the barn door. When I would go out—there was much to see to—the cold struck me as exhilarating, but soon my face felt tight and dead, my nose sharp enough to break and always the bite at the tip. The warmth of my body drew in as a fire dies away into its coals.

The most amazing thing was Ellen's acceptance of the situation. After that first morning she showed me the quality of her courage. Her flurry of despondency had worried me. I expected her to grow difficult. But not at all. She had no thought of herself or of the child she was bearing. It was all for me. She could not do enough for my comfort. She made me tea whenever I came in from the outdoors. She made warm soups and especial dishes I loved. She would rush to get my slippers if my feet were wet and cold. She made me sit by the fire. She would look at me, when I went out, or when I came in, to see if I brought news of any bad luck. How intent was her regard before rushing off to do some errand that would make things more pleasant! She reminded me of those frontier women who molded bullets as they nursed their children. After several days of this I said, "See here, dar-

A NAME FOR EVIL

ling, you treat me as if I were an invalid. I don't deserve it. You are the one things must be done for."

"I'm all right," she said quickly.

"How do you feel?"

"Fine. Fine." And then she would be off as if she had just remembered something that had to be done.

In the evenings, sitting by the fire, she would pick up her sewing and sharpen her eyes on the needle, but I could see her watching to see if I had any wishes that might make the hours pass more pleasantly. There was an element of strain to all this, rather like that between bride and bridegroom when they find themselves, at long last, alone with the separateness of their personalities and need desperately to wipe out the strangeness.

I look back on this as a time, a crucial time, in our lives. I was like the sentinel on a dangerous post who turns from his intense watch to relieve his eyes and rest his spirit at the bright blazing campfire. But what could I do? Ellen was making every effort to show me that the postponement of our departure did not matter. Could I have received this attention coldly and kept to my watch? Such would have been either brutal or heroic, and I was fitted to play neither role. Perhaps I needed this attention more than I thought; perhaps I was done in, exhausted by the continuous vigil. And certainly we had to fill the days and the longer nights, and we had only ourselves to fall back upon. Never had she loved me with so much frenzy, nor had she ever been so lovable. I felt that up to now we had only

207

touched the borders of that dark and passionate grove.

But as the winter, so to speak, dug in I began to feel that something false had crept into our relationship. It was too intense; it could only properly belong to those who die young. It was not the thing to wear out a lifetime. And curiously enough with this awareness came an awareness of change in the aspect of the outside. For the first week the white world seemed beautiful—pure, absolute, bringing respite from the confusion and waste of living. Only in one place was there sign of life. Each day in the barn lot, where the stock was penned, the brown stains left by the cattle spread a little farther, grew a little darker. At first as I passed, I would look away. The lot was the one feature, no more than a speck in the vast whiteness, which marred the purity of what I saw. But it was not long before I found myself eagerly glancing toward it, as to some beacon, on my trips to and from the house.

When we were well on into the second week, the aspect of things had subtly but violently changed. The black poles of the trees stood up out of the white ground, as slick and brittle as on the first morning of the blizzard; the barns and the house stood apart, surrounded, isolated; each object, even the smoke from Johnny's chimney, a thin blue haze rising straight up, seemed caught in the air. But it was no longer the whiteness. It was the stillness now which made the disunity of this solitude.

In the room where I kept a great fire going, and it was a cheerful fire, the flames bending over the back stick, changing color as the heat became great or small, even here, just beyond the circle of the hearth the cold waited in the room, and the quiet there was the same quiet that had settled everywhere over our world. One would pass through it to the fire; the heat might even drive it from the room; but one had only to open the . door and there it was, in the next room, filling the air, waiting. . . . Just as somewhere about, in some bleak corner, or in the wide open ways, there was one particular spot of air colder, more quiet, but also waiting. . . .

And then toward the last of the third week the white fog drifted in.

CHAPTER THIRTY-ONE

*M*Y FIRST thought was: it will
thaw now. My next thought
was of Ellen. I must tell her.
After all, disguise it as she had, she desperately wanted
to go away to have the child. I made her dress and
then wrap up in her warmest things, without telling
her why. It seemed a foolish game to play, but I did
not want her to discover the fog for herself. I wanted
to show it to her. "But why so mysterious?" she asked.
"Never mind," I said. "You will see."

Once outdoors I said, "Look. Isn't it beautiful?"
And I waved my hand as if I had ordered it as a special
gift for her.

She caught her breath. "It is beautiful. But why
did you want to bring me out in it?"

We were walking toward the garden.

"I wanted to be the first to show you. The weather
is changing. Soon I can take you away."

"Oh really, darling." Her voice choked ever so little.

We walked on. I opened the garden gate and we
paused just inside.

"How lovely the garden is!" she said. "And how
unreal!"

I saw what she meant. All the imperfections left

by time had been covered. We seemed to be adrift in a white cloud, in some unknown ideal place, where we were the only inhabitants. The snow and ice had perfected the bordering hedges. The flowering bushes which, in summer, showed a few scraggly buds, now presented to our gaze the absolute proportions, the subdued glitter, of one blooming mass. Our feet crunched the walkways. The outlines of the paths were faintly visible; and along them we followed the circle within the circle, confining the fanlike beds. We wandered here and there. Once behind the white air the garden wall wavered like a shadow. Except for the soft crunching steps there was no sound. We moved in utter silence. The air was become silence at last made visible. Our solitude was complete.

"The glare no longer pinches my eyes," Ellen said.

"There's no glare here," I replied. "Wouldn't it be wonderful if, with a wave of the hand, we could make the summer garden as perfect as this? And once perfected, drench it in some such arresting atmosphere?"

"We can do it. Or almost," she said. "But not with a wave of the hand."

"No, not with a wave of the hand."

And then we found ourselves near the springhouse. It rose up into the fog like a monument, all its rotting structure transformed.

"Let's not go too near," she said softly. "Let them rest in peace."

"Always you think of those women," I said.

"I feel very close to them now," she answered. And

then after a little, in some panic, "Which way is the gate?"

I put her arm in mine. "Don't fret. I know the way out."

She drew away. "But where is it? One could wander here for hours. I've heard of such things." She turned around and pointed, one way and then another, and I saw that her alarm was real.

"Don't get excited. I'll take you out."

I reached for her hand.

"No, no," she cried. "I'll wait here. I know where I am here. You find the gate and call me. I'll come."

I was torn between staying and going. To leave her in such a state seemed a kind of abandonment. I must calm her. But she would not hear of me staying. "Go! Go!" she said.

It was apparent I must end this condition of affairs as quickly as possible. To remain another instant might set forever the mark of terror in her eyes. In my haste I moved blindly into the fog. It was then, swallowed up by it, I found that in my solicitude for her I had lost direction. I stopped and looked every way into the white deep air, and every way it opened up but only to show itself. The solid whiteness had usurped the air. There was no center, no four points of the compass. Within the circle the circle had come to an end.

But I knew there was a gate and, feeling now myself some panic, I began to run, trusting to blind chance. I quickly enough came up against the wall, but it was the unbroken wall I touched. Time and again I retraced my steps, approached it by the next path, but always the gate eluded me. And everywhere the trodden snow and everywhere the motionless depth of the fog, the cold dull white cloud of it, and beyond it the hard substance of the wall, surrounding us, confining us, the little gap closed up. Then at one certain moment I discovered my center of being had become the nameless dread which lurks in dreams, is known but may not be named.

In this white blindness I reached to my forehead and brushed away the clammy sweat. Should I call out to Ellen and terrify her? Not yet certainly. Instead, slowly I trod the crystal floor, looking down, fearing now the effluvium which had replaced the air and which at first had seemed so beautiful.

So it happened that in this latter stage of my bewilderment the fog took from me the sense of time.

But remembering the woodsman's trick, I began myself to move in a circle, carefully widening it. This was a last resort. It might bring me back to Ellen. There was no other way now. Together again we could wait until Johnny came to feed the stock. If I shouted, he might hear me. But when would that be? Would the dark blot out this whiteness? Would Johnny feed early and slip back to his house before I could call? Once together again, I would explain to Ellen, and like a foghorn I would call out at intervals.

Treading the circle I had made, something, some intuition, made me lift my eyes from my tracks. There she was, barely visible in the opaque light, directly in front of me. She had not heard me come up. She stood with her head slightly bent, in the frozen tension of one who looks down into an abyss. Her hands were clasped over her bosom. I felt a boundless relief, but as I looked more sharply I saw that she was listening to no spoken words, but to some secret communication she was well practiced in deciphering. The whole appalling truth was before me.

"Ellen!" I screamed.

My anguish and the fixity of my purpose to save her gave to my cry its unearthly quality. She bounded forward, whirled around and, looking blindly at me, made the sound of a wounded beast. And then she saw me. For one instant she turned upon me a wild, transforming stare, when she began to back slowly away, moaning, "No, no, no," over and over again.

"Stop! It's me," I called out.

But she did not stop. It was then I saw toward what she was moving. A few steps away, on the platform of the springhouse stood my enemy, waiting. There was no need to look but in my instantaneous glance I saw that he was dressed as a bridegroom. And I saw his face, the hateful features I had come to know as well as my own, triumph and desire shining out of the hollow eyes. And then the two long arms reached forth.

"You shall not!" I shouted and dashed forward.

But I was a fraction of a moment too late. With a lightness she could not have managed alone Ellen leaped upon the platform where she was awaited. I heard a crackling of timbers, a long crash, and there before my eyes she and Major Brent disappeared into the depths below.

I tore open the old trap door, half ran, half slid down the rotten steps. I stood in the inner darkness of the pit, sinking up to my ankles in the oozing muck which for years had stopped up the spring's mouth. From above, where the floor had broken through, a dull light penetrated into the gloom—enough for me to make out the heap lying in front of me. With a cry of hope I knelt, I gathered her into my arms. Oh, with what passion I held her! Carefully now I whispered her name. She was slow to answer. Hoarsely I shouted it, but the round walls of the slimy pit, not she, gave back the lifeless word. Desperately my eyes reached for the light to make it show me her face. The light hovered, like a stain of breath, below the break in the floor. I saw it cast no reflection, but I saw this without surprise. Already I knew what it was I held in my arms, and I knew that at last I was alone.

Date